AUDUBON PARK

EXERCISE, GATHER, ENJOY THE BEAUTY!

Nat Fleck

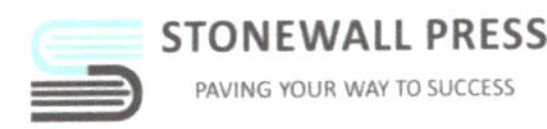

STONEWALL PRESS

PAVING YOUR WAY TO SUCCESS

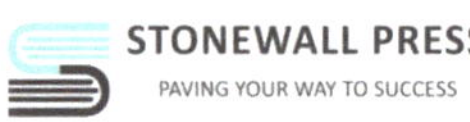

Published by Stonewall Press
4800 Hampden Lane
Suite 200, Bethesda, MD 20814 USA
www.stonewallpress.com
1-888-334-0980

Audubon Park

Exercise, Gather, Enjoy the Beauty!

Come and visit this beautiful urban park in New Orleans. Find peace in the fields or by the lagoon or the so large Mississippi River. See all the wild and crazy, fun and funky, things we do in it every day. Enjoy all of the wildlife.

Pictures and text from

Fotos by Fleck

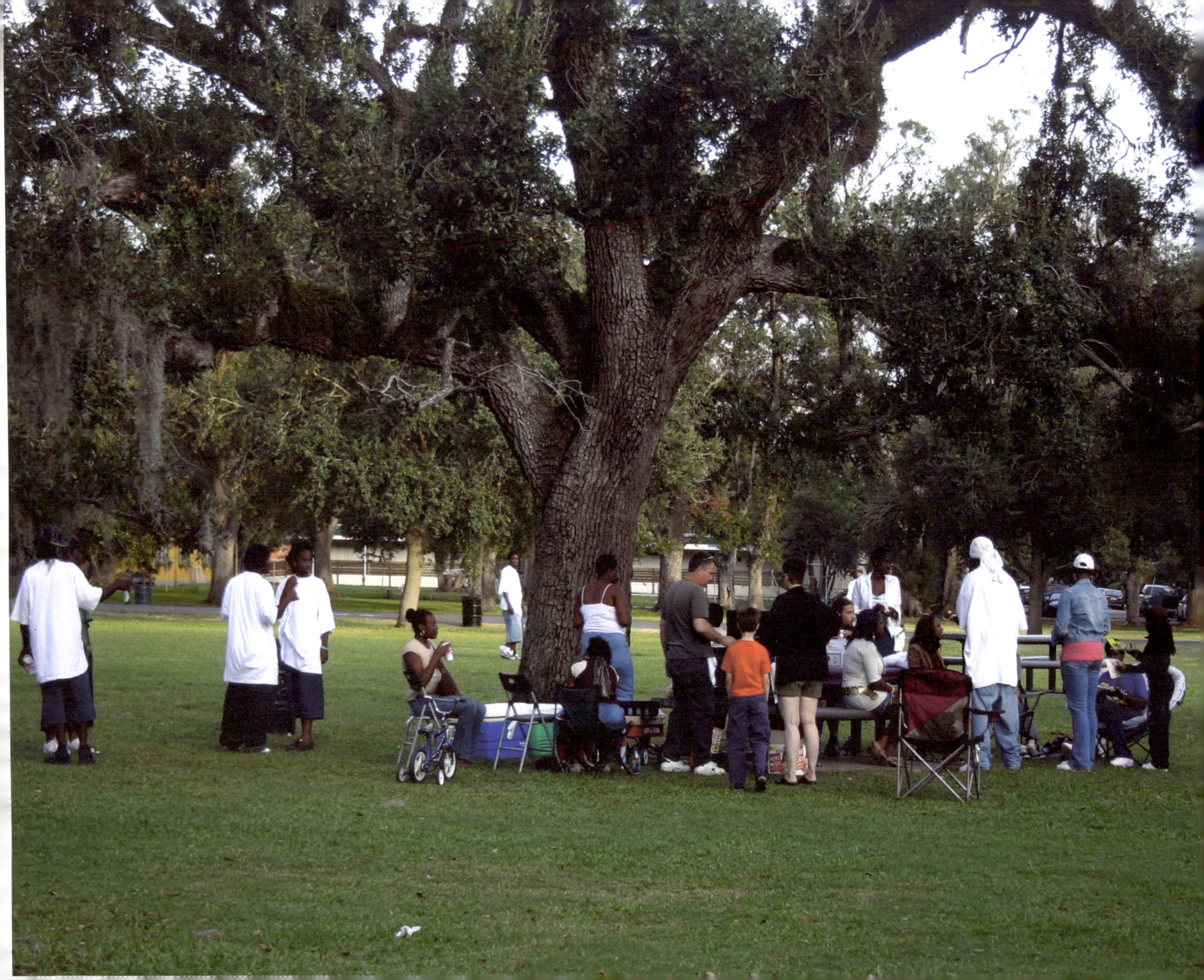

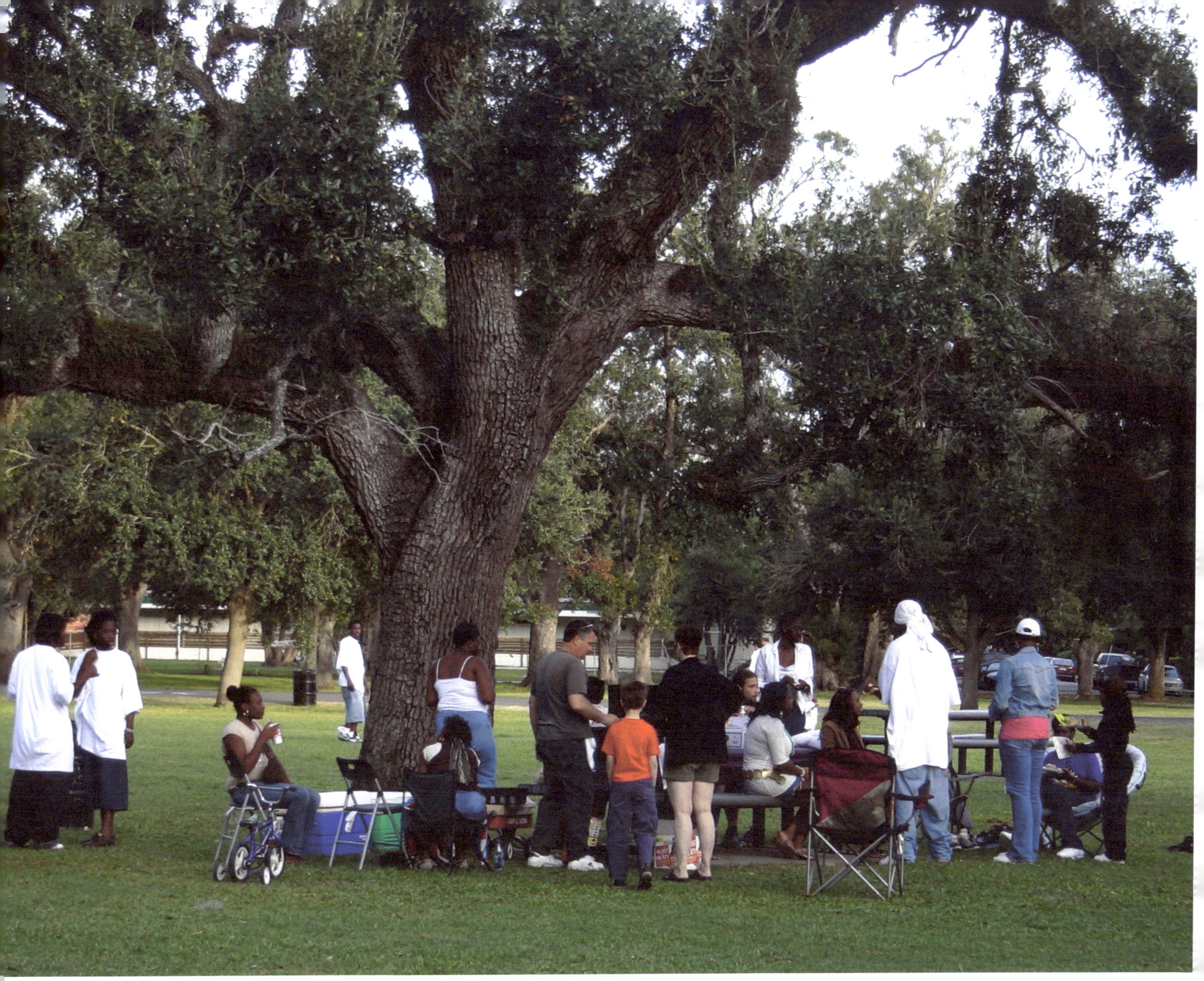

Audubon Park: partly natural, mostly not…

What is an urban park? What is this urban park? To me, an urban park is mostly defined or identified by what goes on in it.

This park is all about activity. It is a whole village of activities from the frenetic and frantic to the quiet and meditative. Much of the activity takes place on a paved passageway that circles the park near its perimeter. The backdrop to these activities are large flowing oak branches some of which create a tunnel over the passageway. Alongside that passageway halfway around is a lagoon that seems to rise and fall and open and close each season. In the lagoon is a wide range of natural life: fish, Wood Ducks, other ducks, geese and water birds live there, some raising families. Turtles, squirrels, and even an alligator live in or around the lagoon. We come to sit by the water and to feed the ducks. Hawks call from overhead. Flowers abound.

The rest of the passageway is flanked by a golf course with hill and water features created by us and occupied by gulls, egrets, ibises and other birds along, of course, with the golf players. On the passageway are all sorts of propulsion devices either to help reduce exercise or to enhance it. It seems that our lives are so out of balance that we have to make or unmake exercise. It is fun to see all of the different ways that that happens. Even the golf players do not walk anymore!

Around the park on the outside of the passageway are fields for play or relaxation or rehearsal and so much more. There are shelters and play equipment and trees for climbing.

People come to the park for so many reasons. Some play golf and some come to picnic. Many bring their children to play. Some come to see the turtles or watch the ducks. Some come to be outside and to feel and hear the sounds of the country in this little village in the city. Others have their headphones so they do not have to hear the sounds of the village. Some come for peace and soft light. Some come to run or to kick a ball. For me, going to the park is like going to the zoo; there are a lot of strange and fun and usual and unusual activities all melded into this one ballet. All of us performing at once in the common space!

Audubon Park is a place of natural beauty with so much fun and so many different performances on so many different stages. I hope I have captured some of it here.

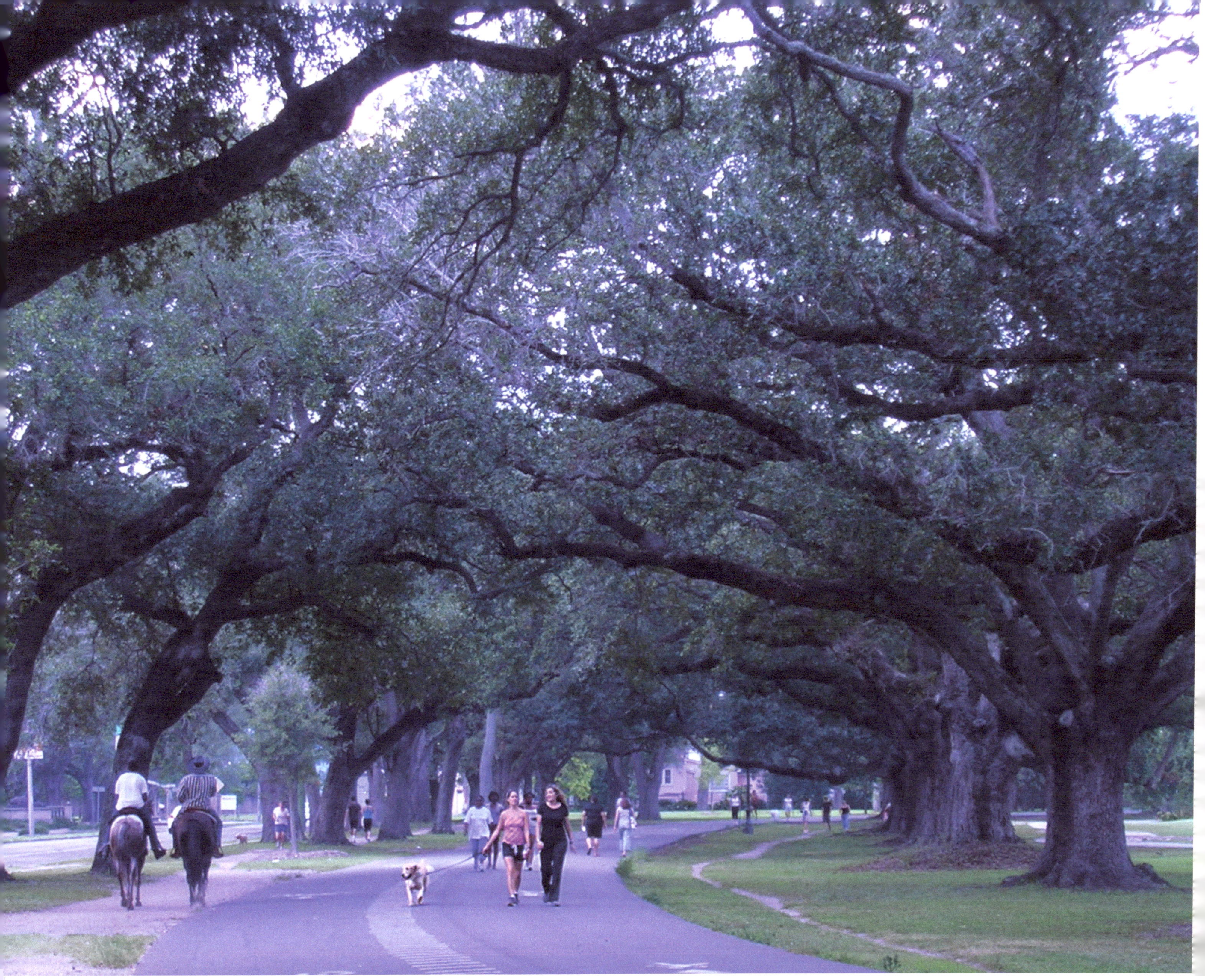

What do we see as we walk around the park?... Action, Scenery, Quietude

ON THE ROAD & ON THE LAWNS... so many scenarios: Hey Daddy keep pedaling while I read. Chatting on the cell while walking or running or biking or skating in the park. Lots of kids tooling around the park on all sorts of contraptions or climbing in the trees or on the slide. Parties, parties, parties. Lots of gatherings! And of course, adults pushing, pulling, carrying kids. And some of that in front of grand southern homes… And then there are those wheeled vehicles.

VISTAS… the morning air is cool and the dew is on the golf course. Behind stands the steeple of the church at Loyola. The view (on the cover) across the golf course can be magical. The oaks, around the park and over the road, framing so much of the activity can be mesmerizing. The ducks, the geese, the swan in the lagoon or the turtles on a log draw me to the park. It is such a special oasis in the city.

PEACE… It can be so quiet. I see someone walking through the oaks to infinity or resting on a bench. I hear the Tree Ducks whistling. A hawk whistles overhead. I start to relax. Is that "Country Roads, take me home" I hear? John Denver? No, it is the group by the road with the guitar. Now I hear a song from Nova Scotia. This has been a long walk; I am in the maritime provinces! Oh no, again; now it is the foursome singing a maritime ditty. Maybe the next corner will bring me something cajun…

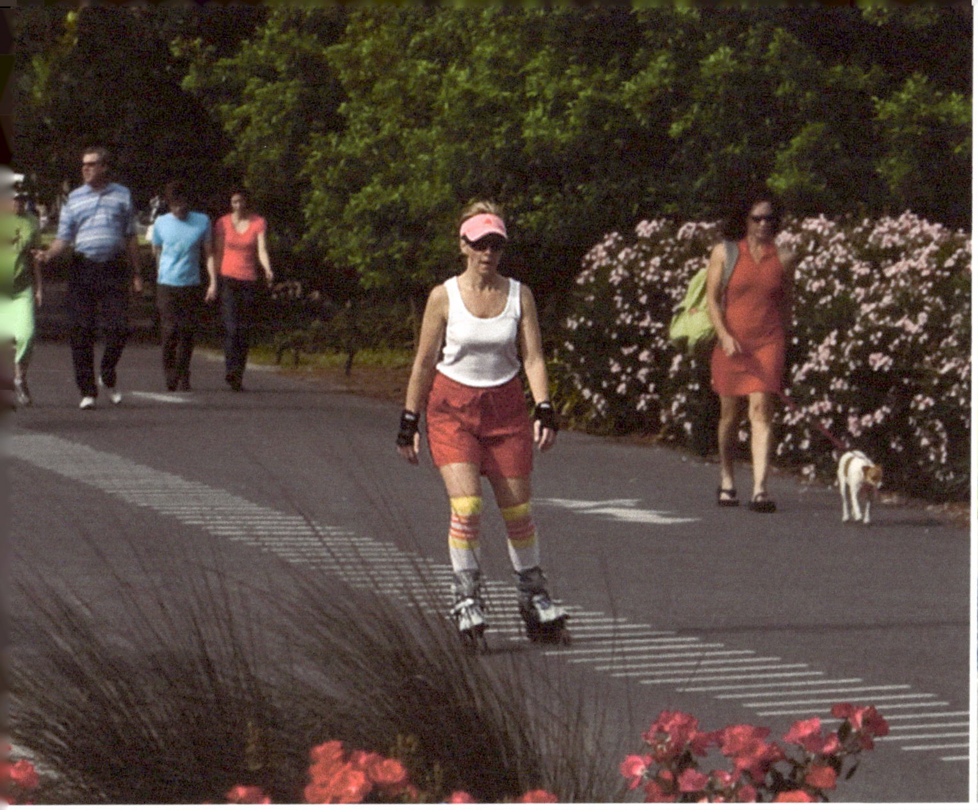

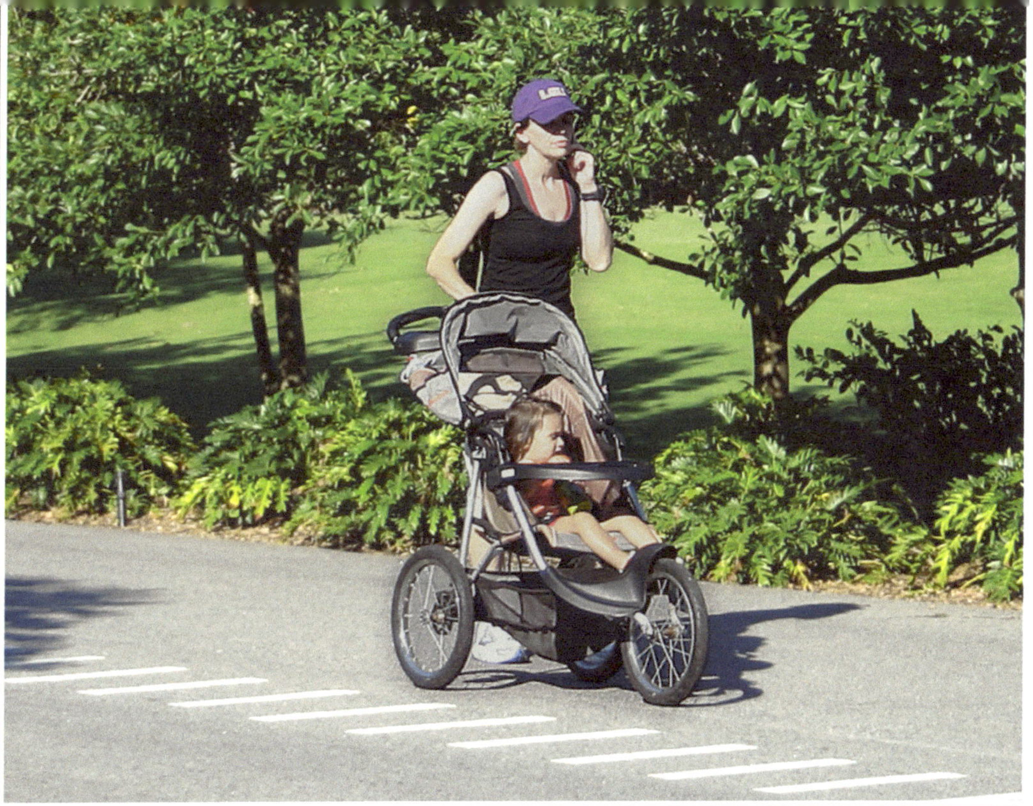

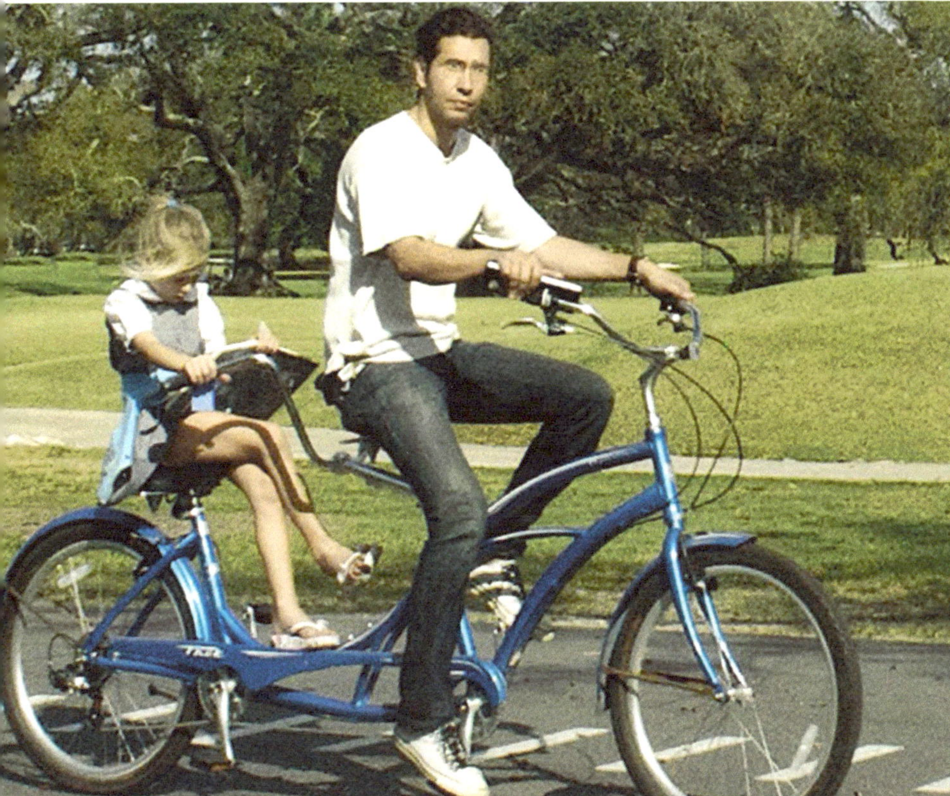
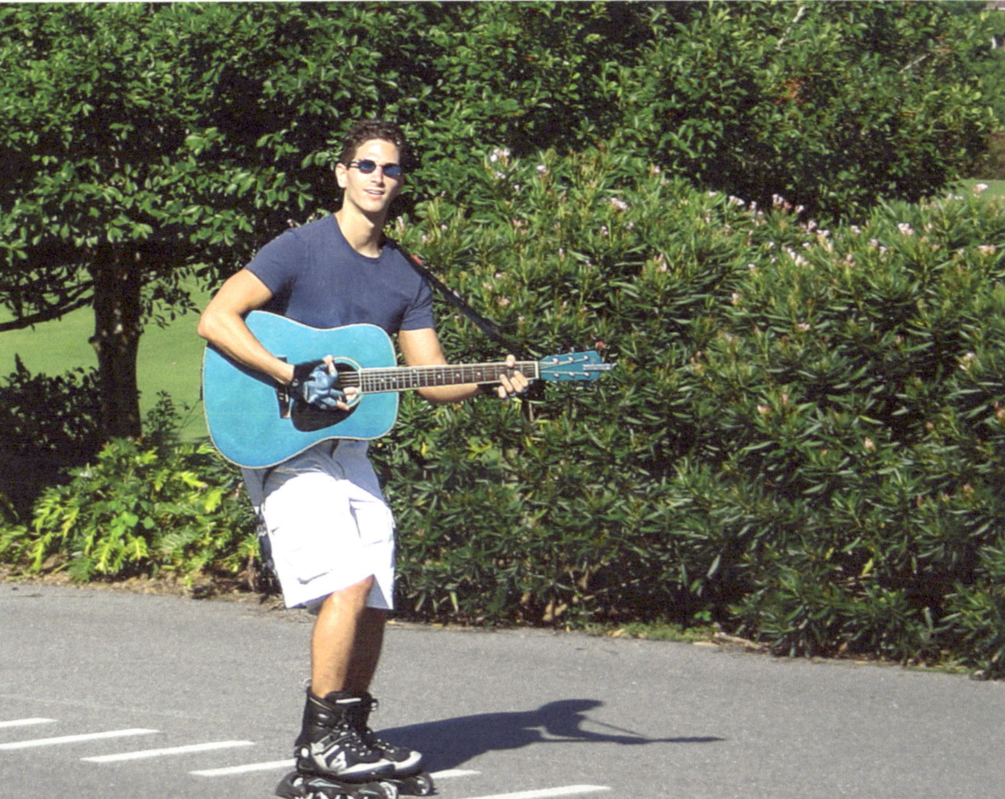

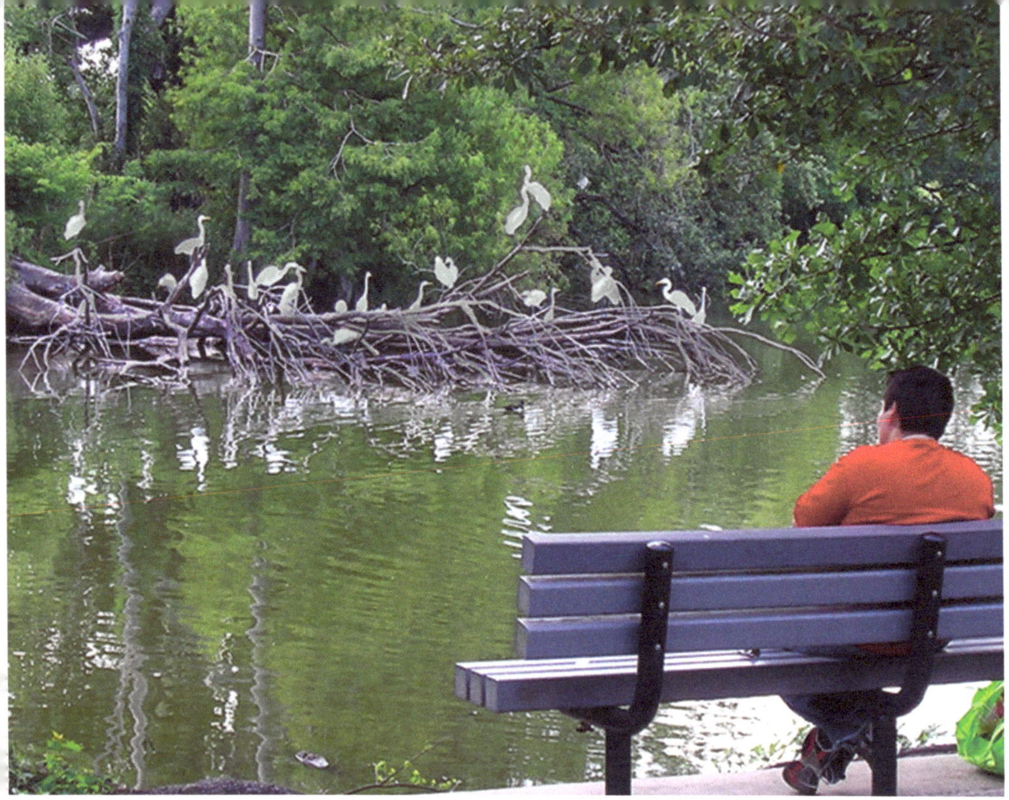

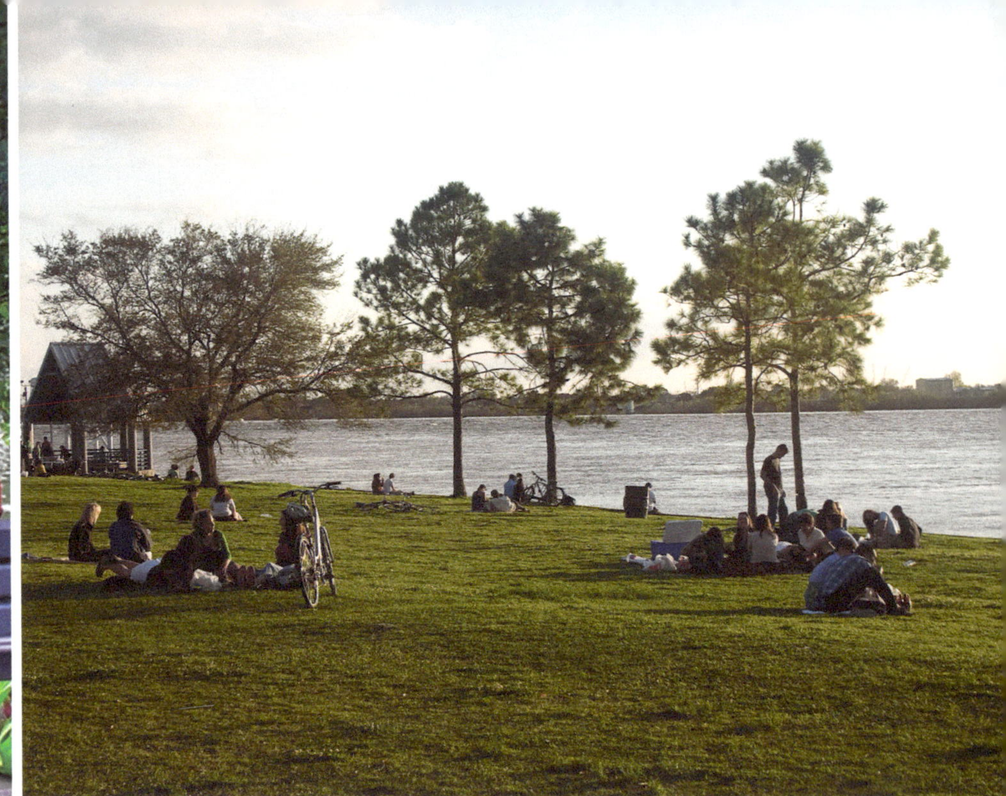

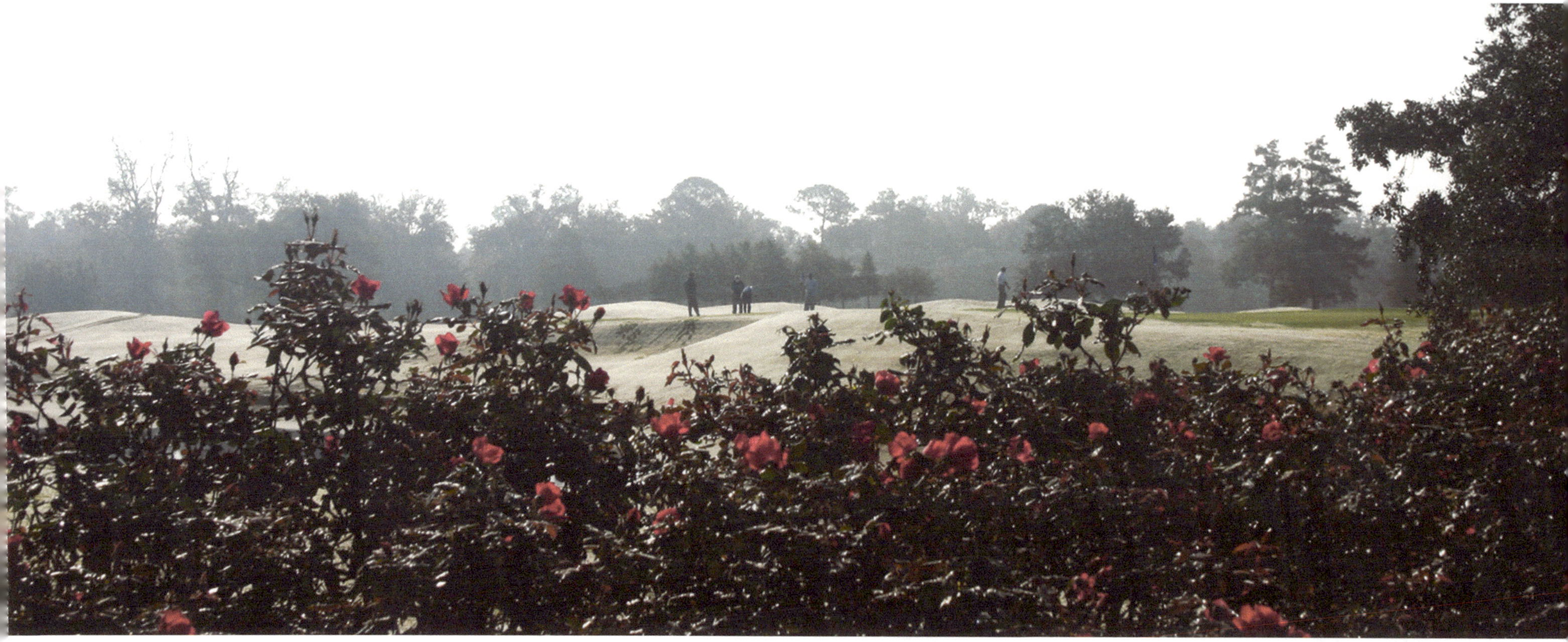

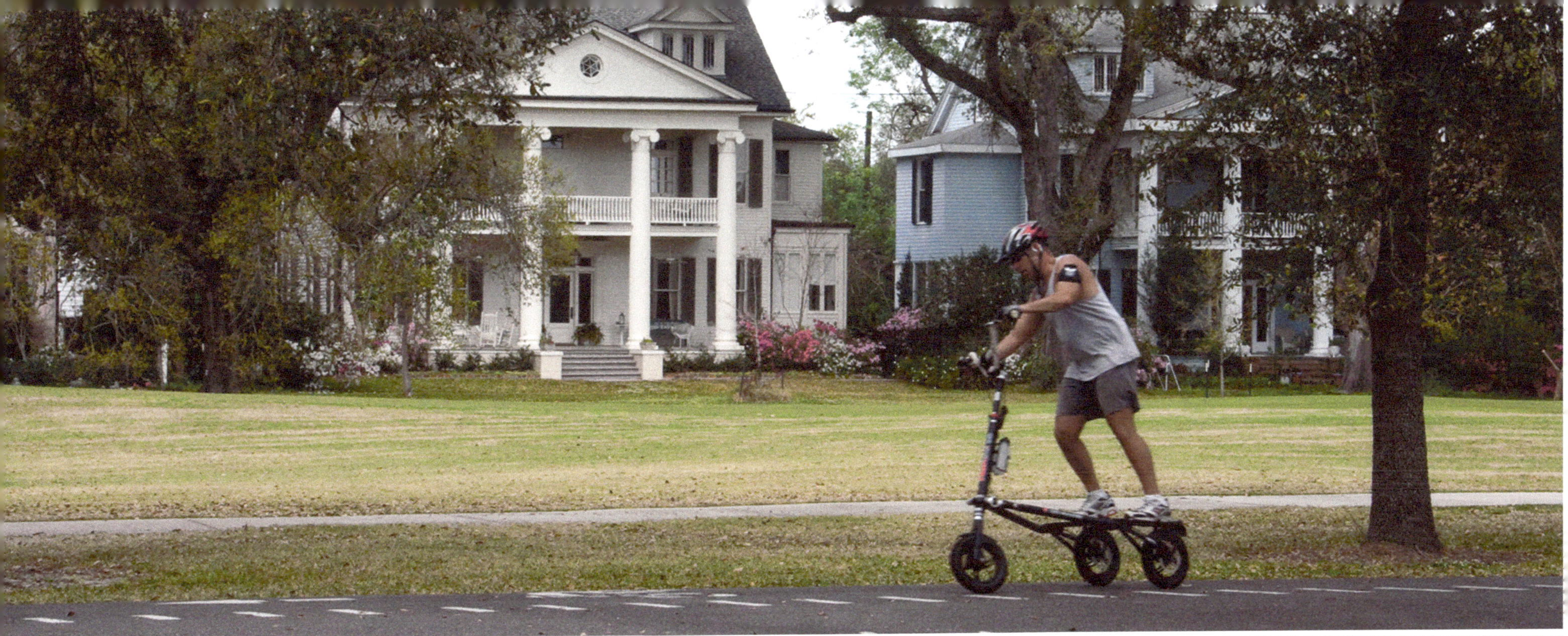

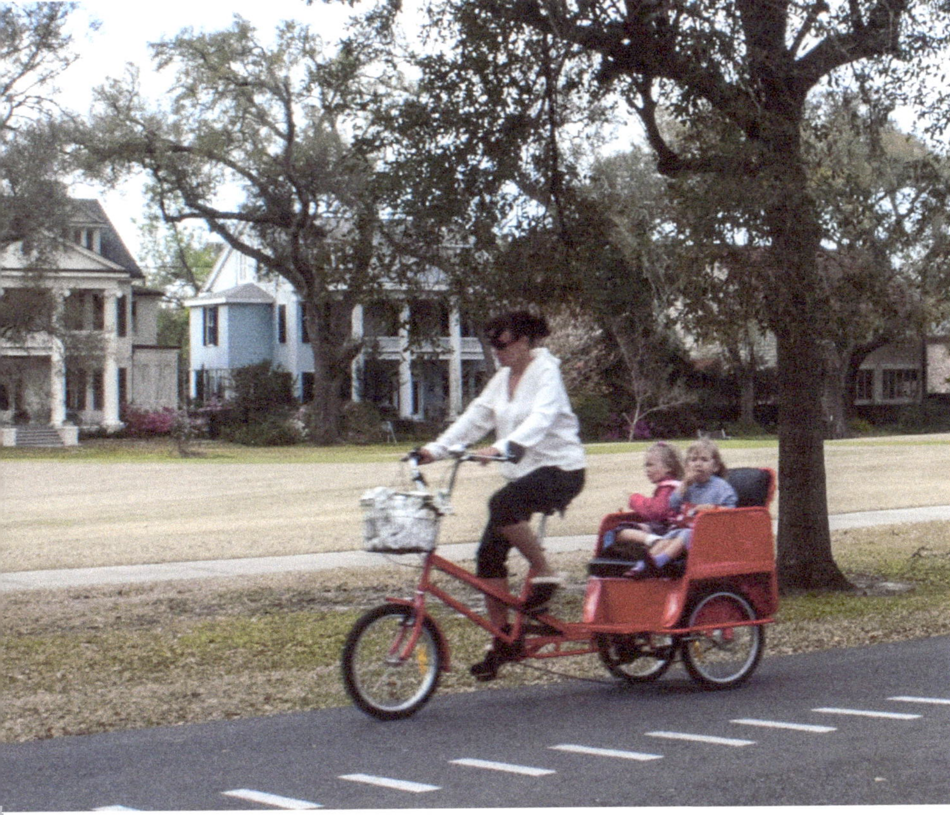
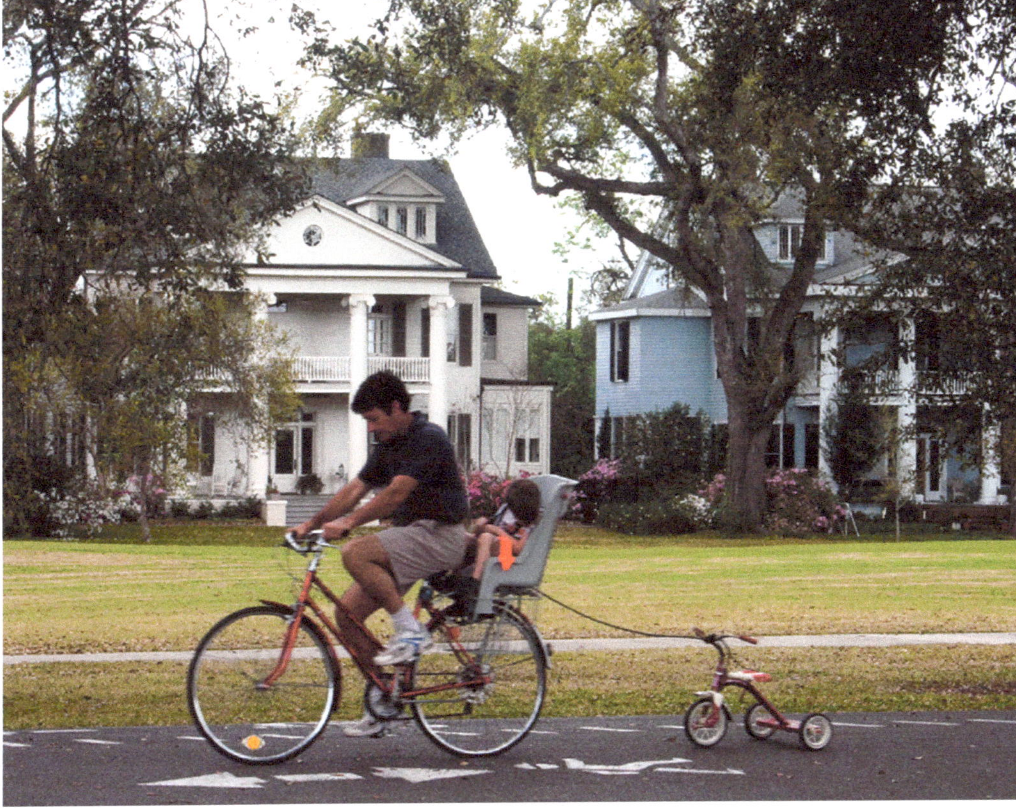

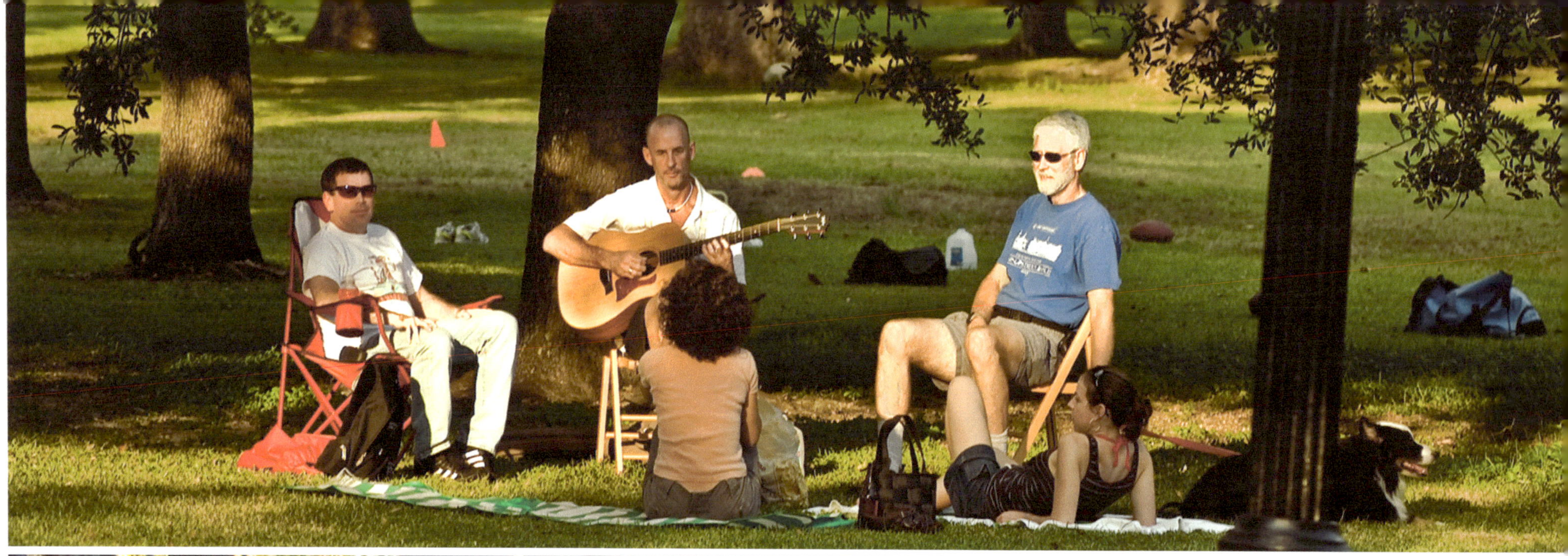

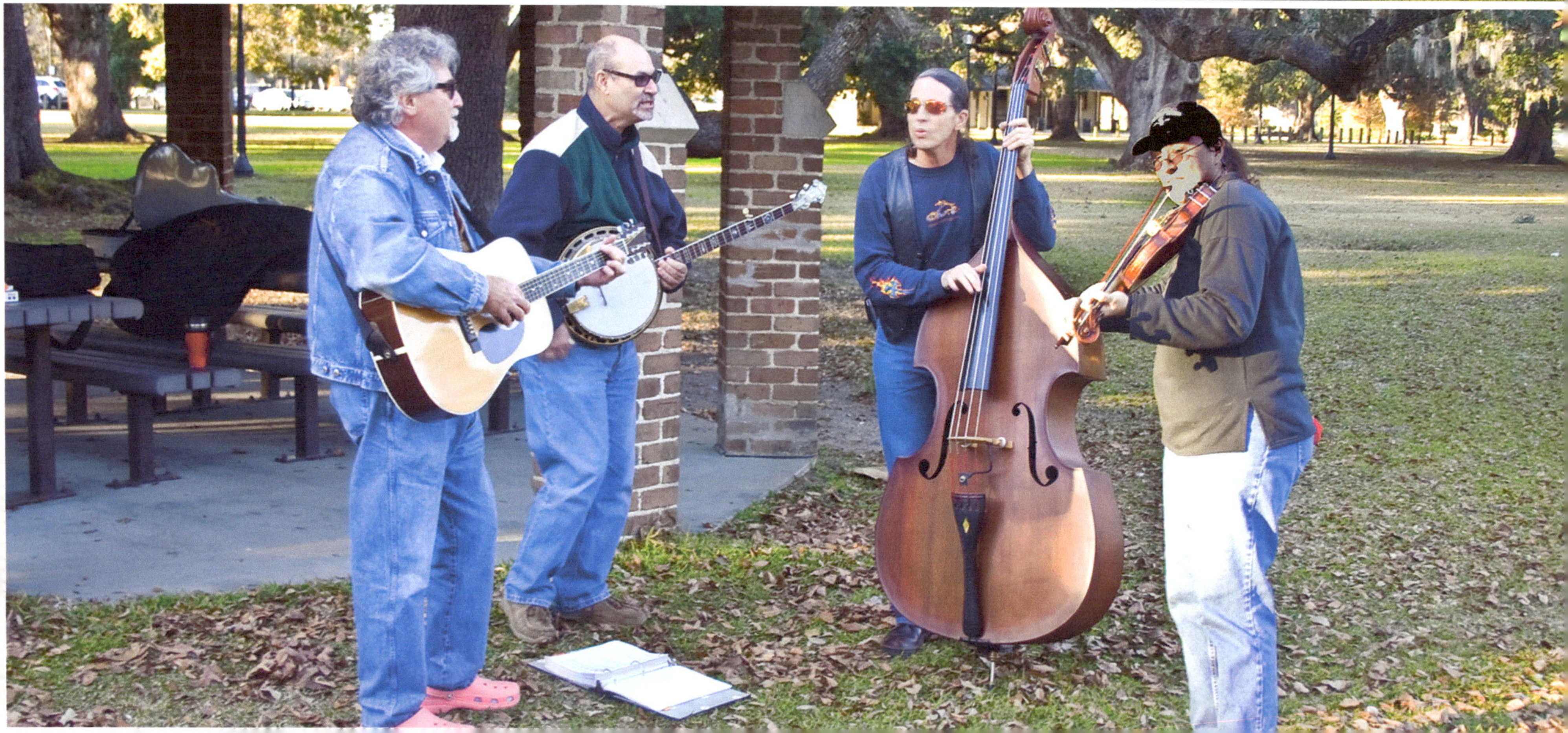

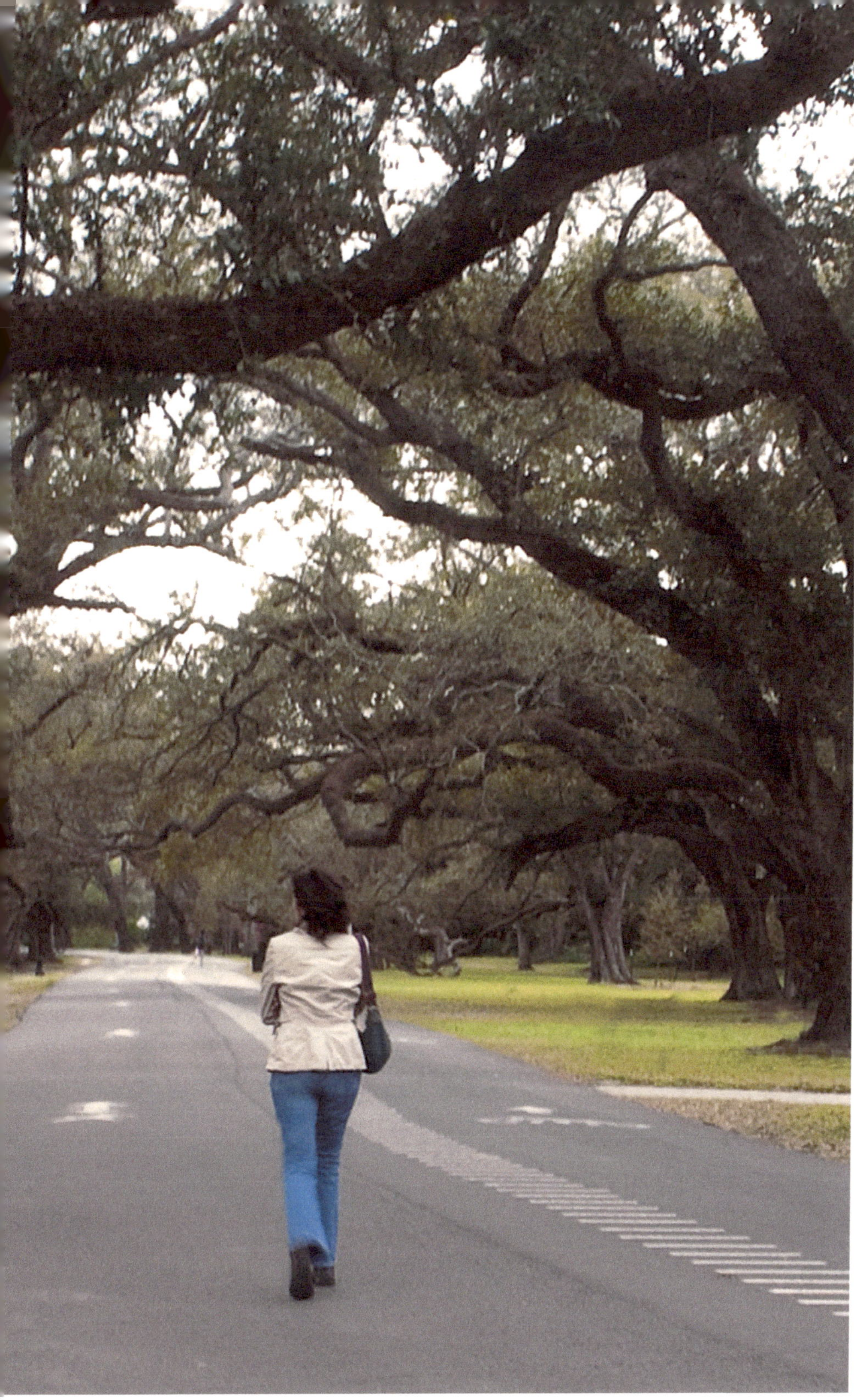

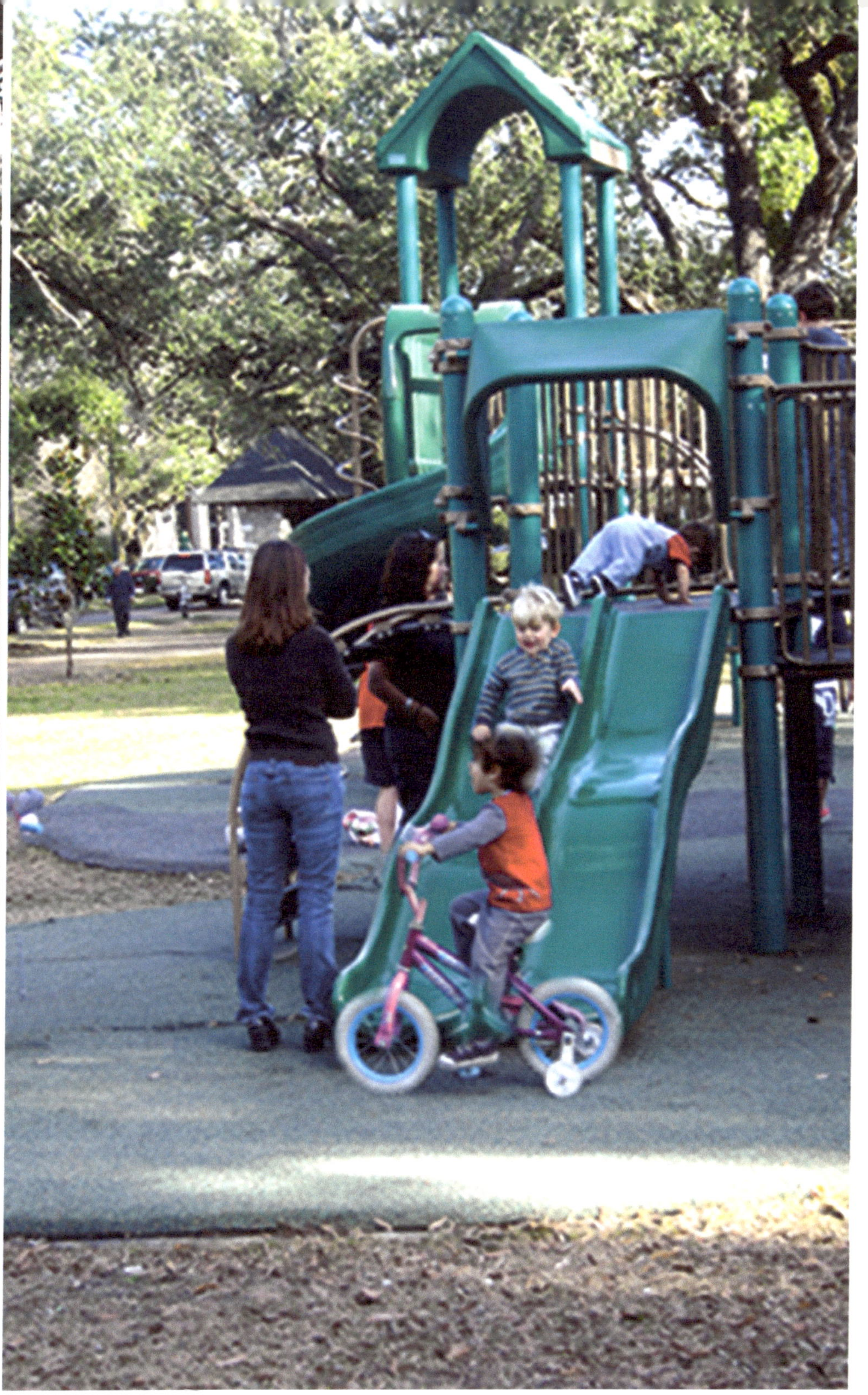

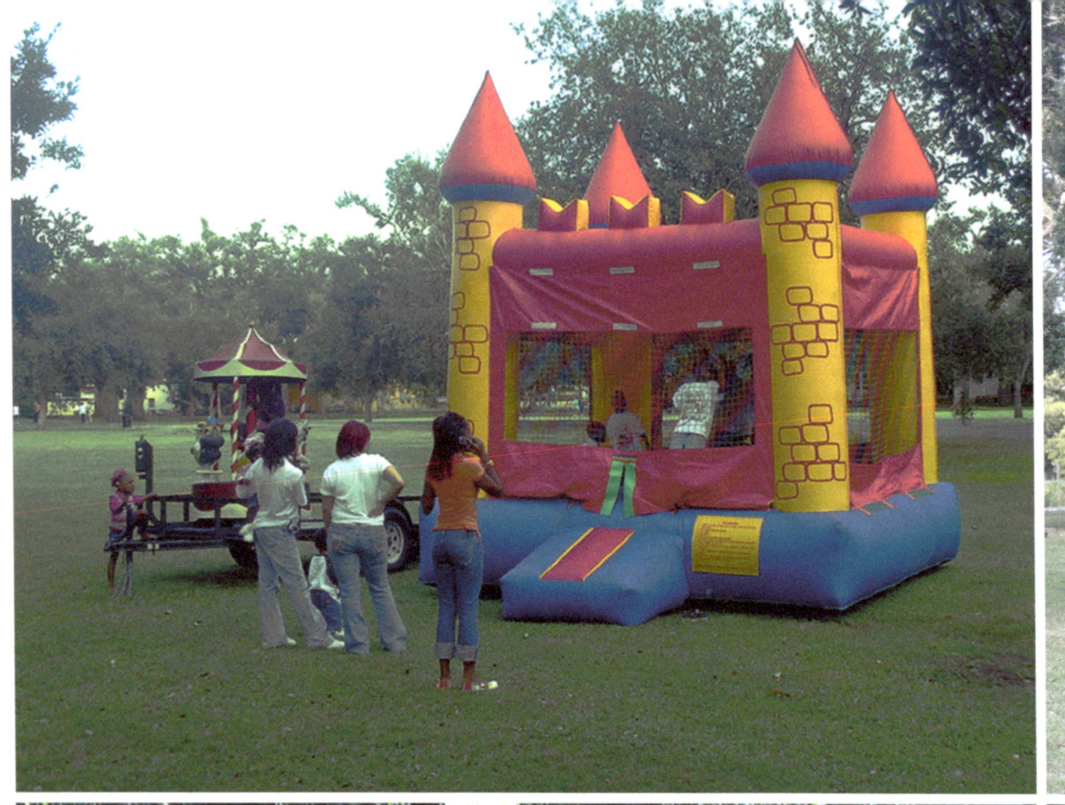
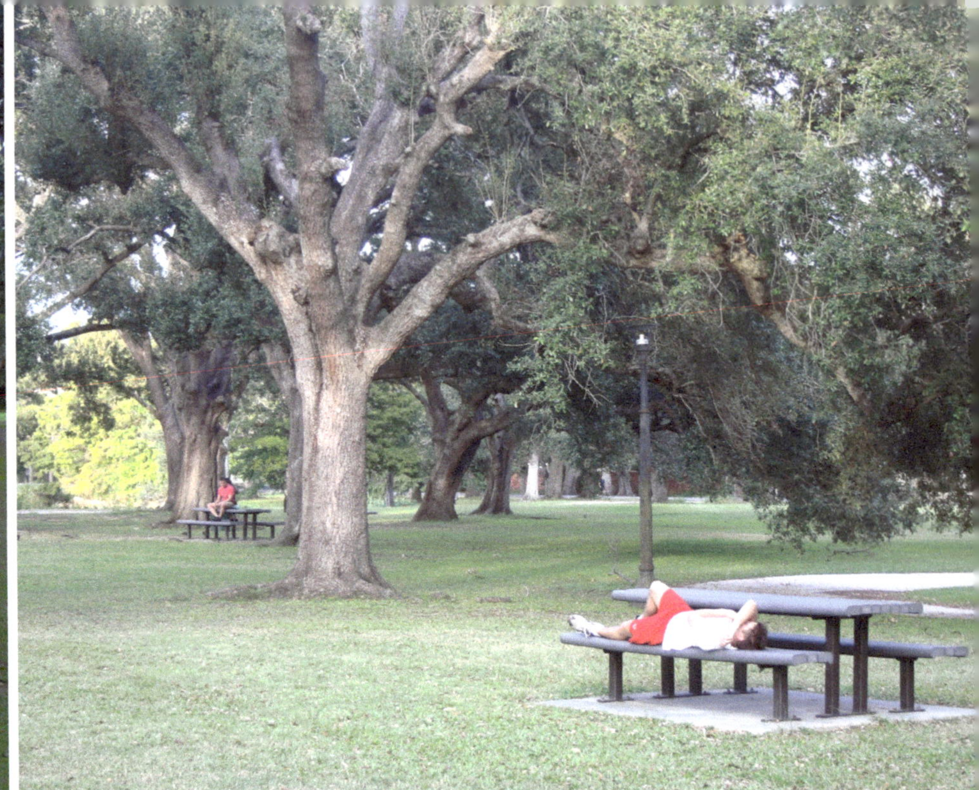
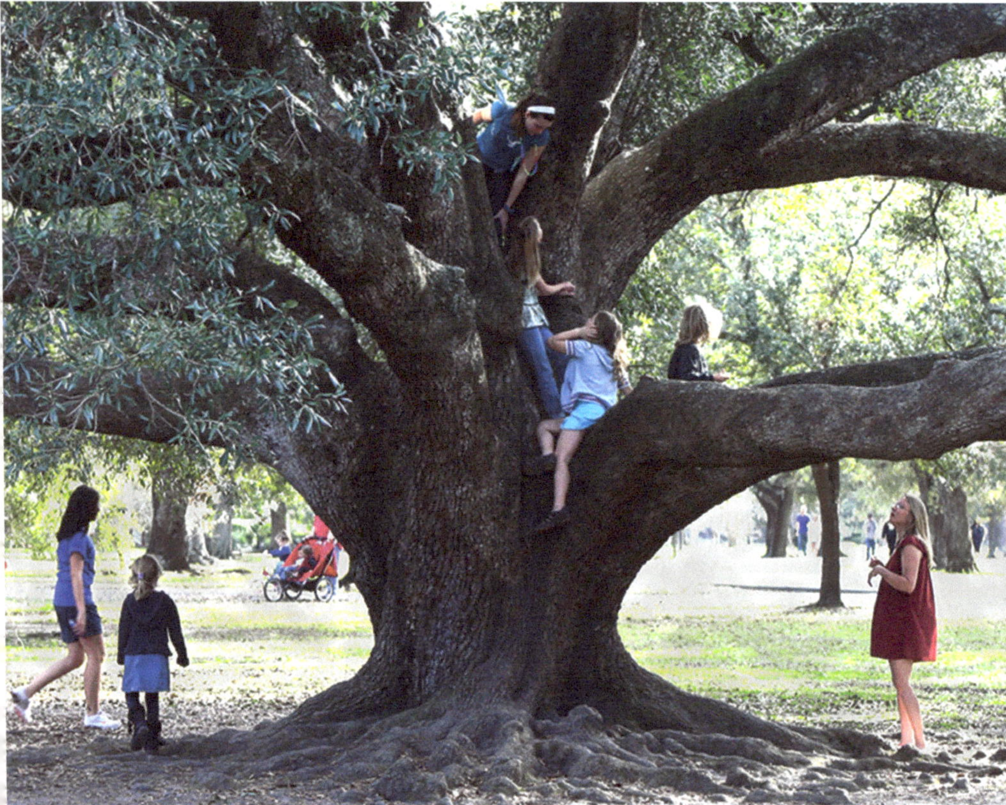
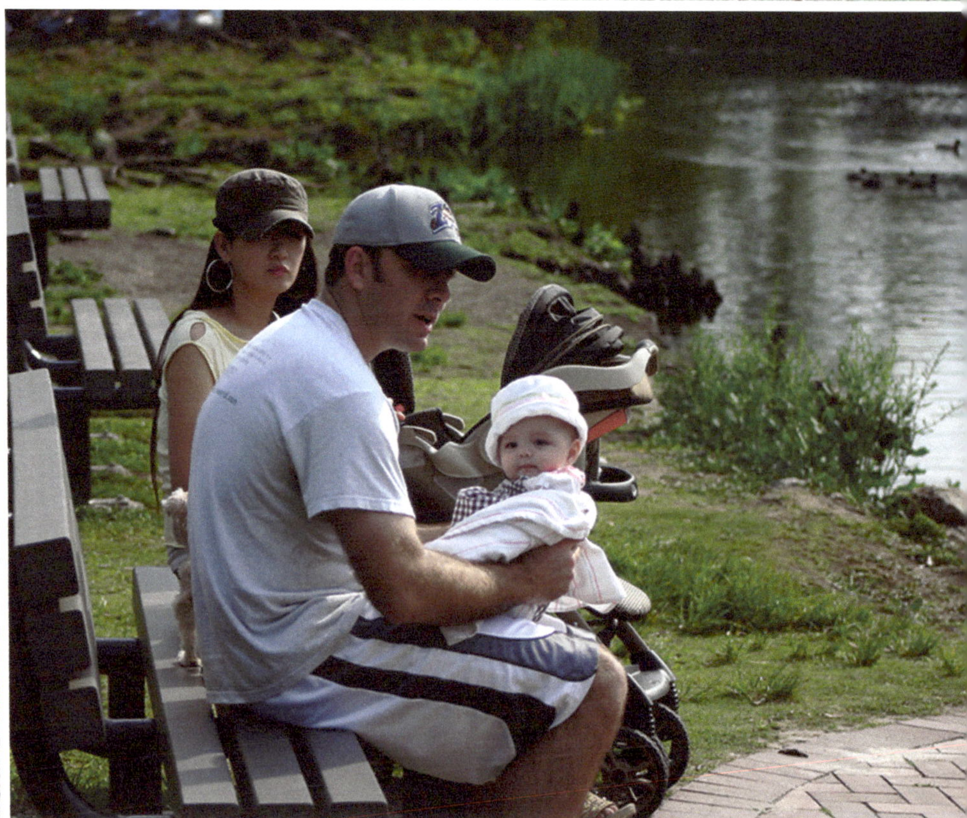

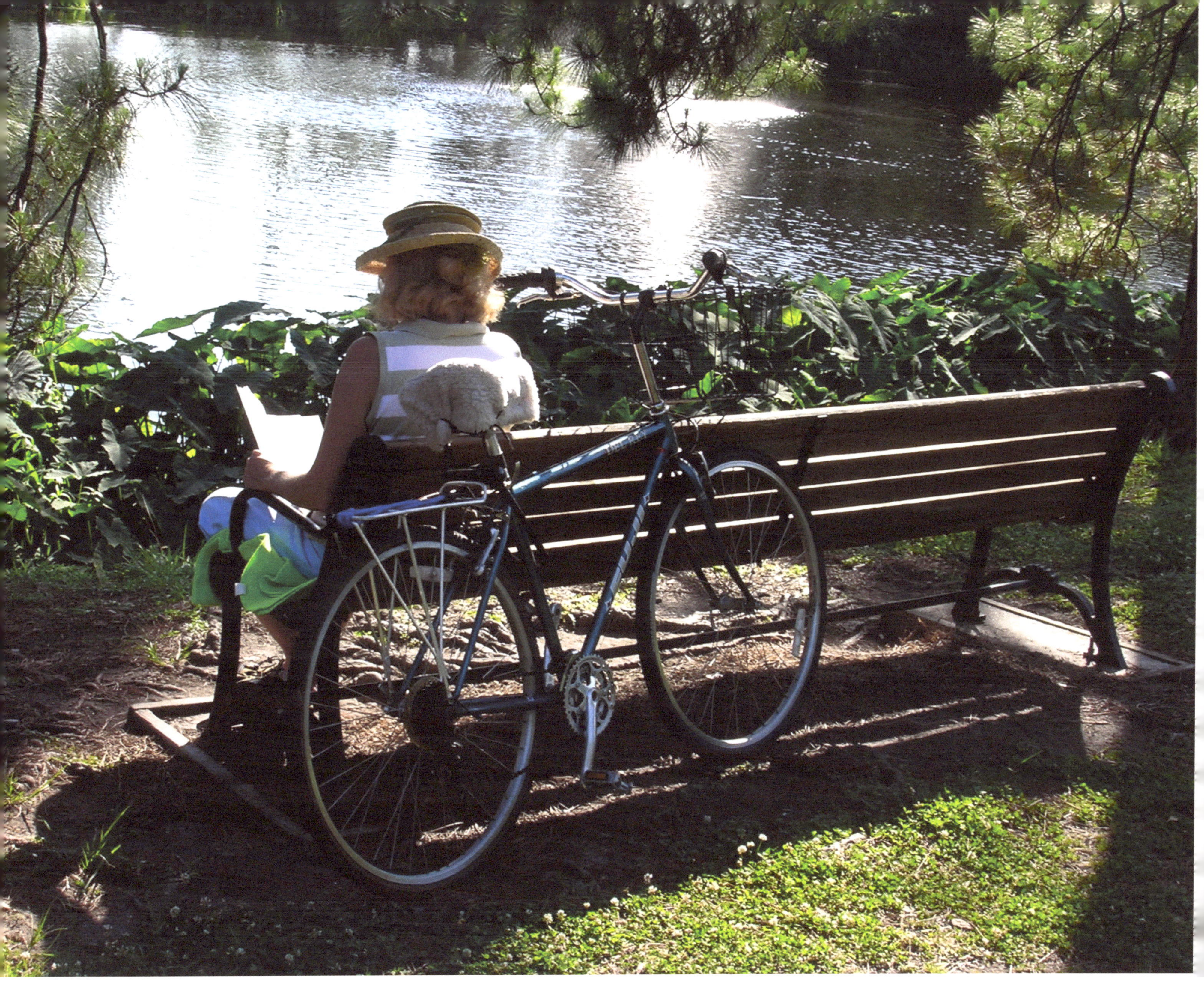

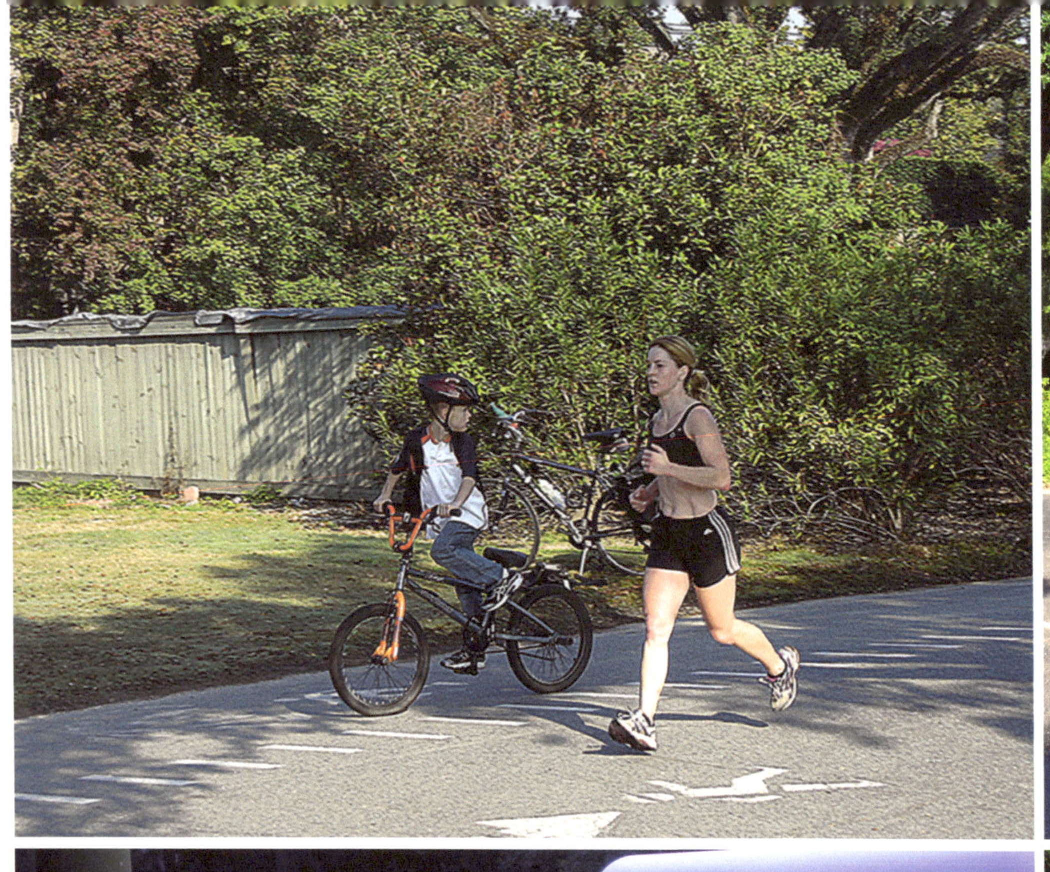
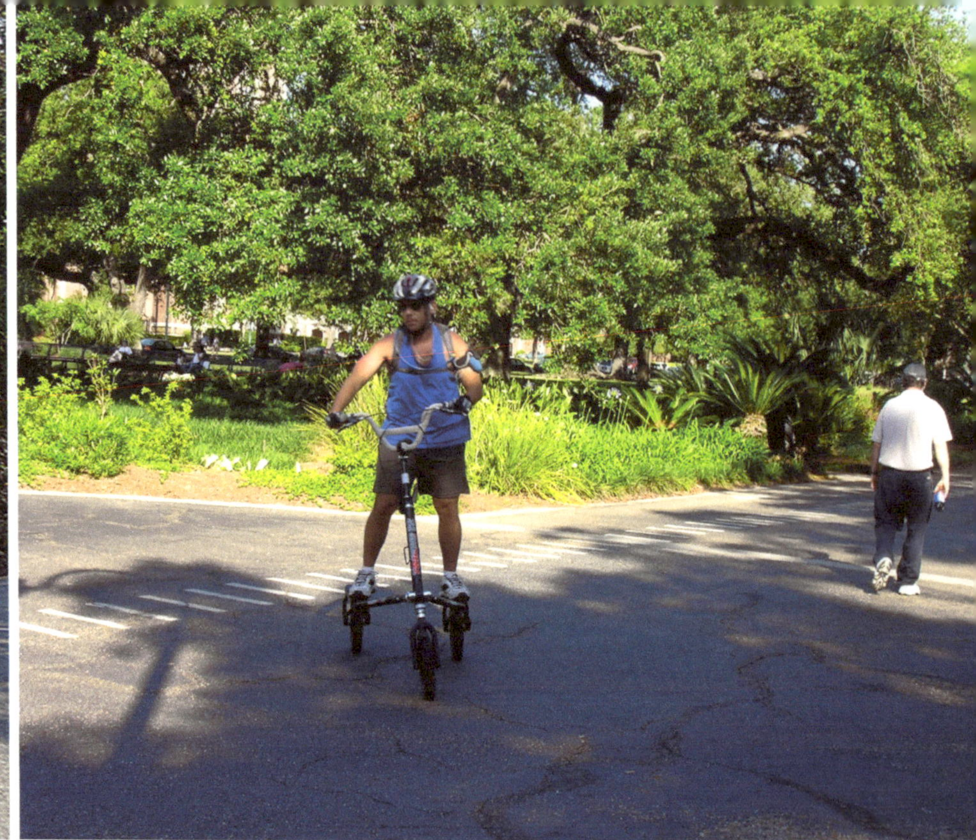
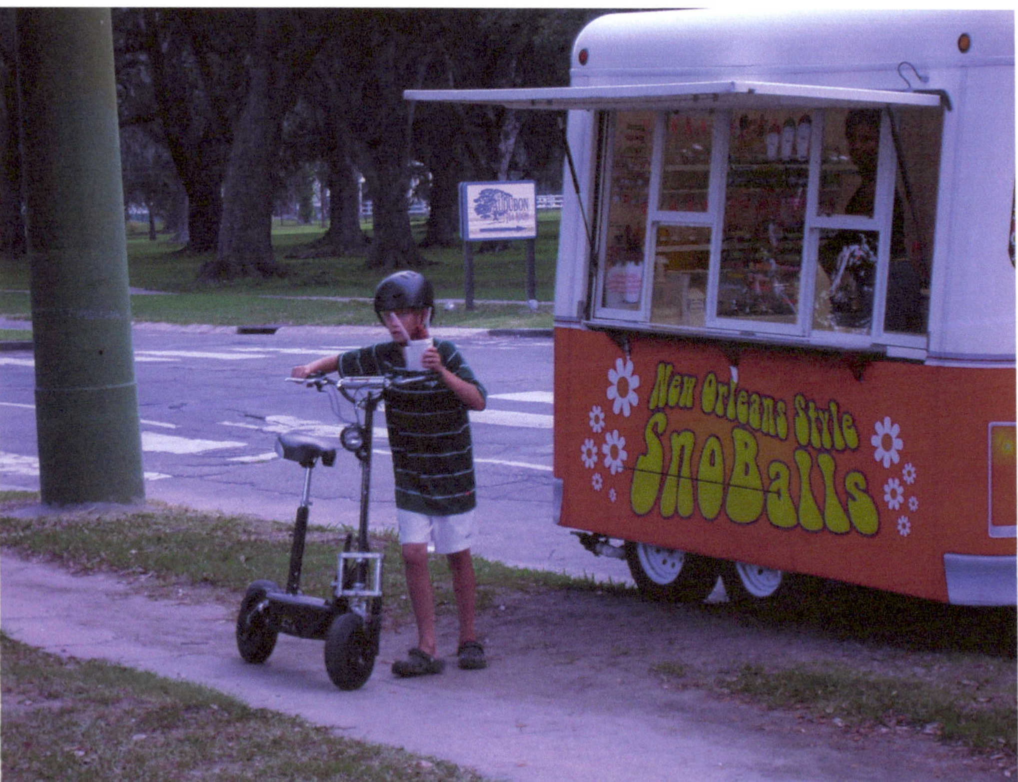
New Orleans Style
SnoBalls
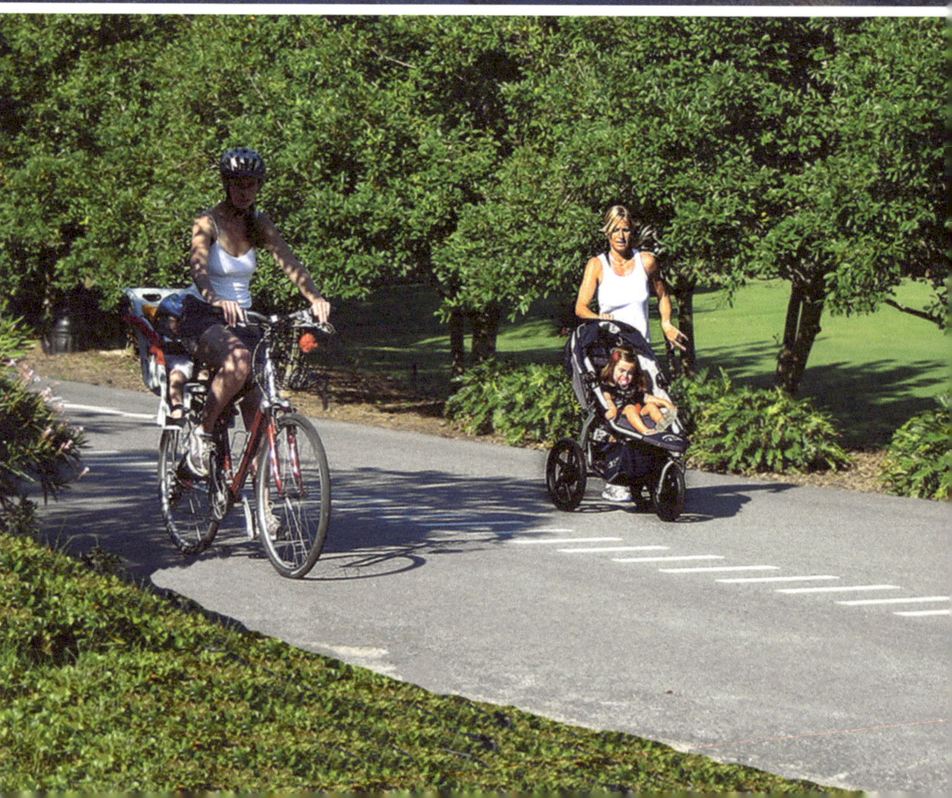

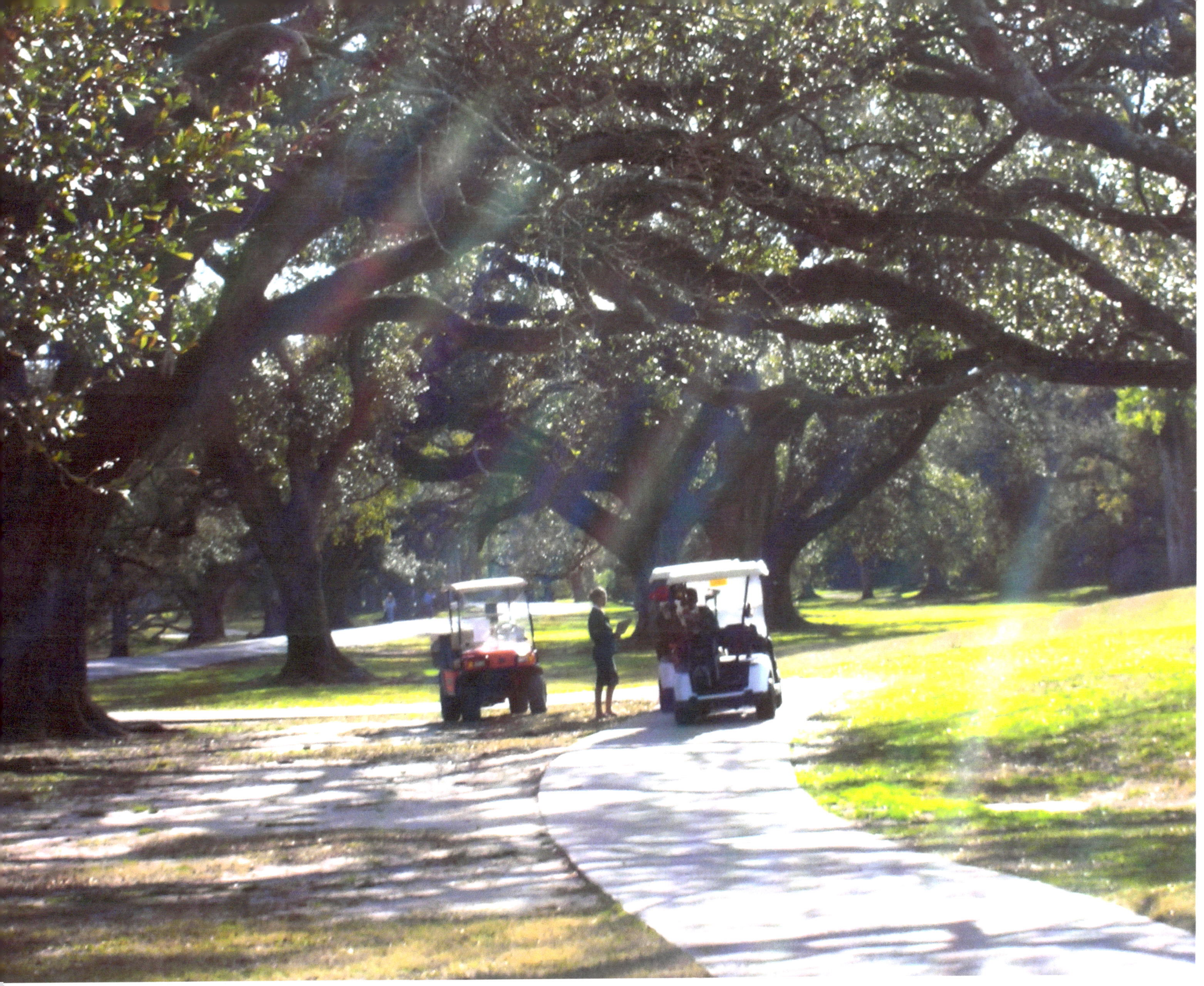

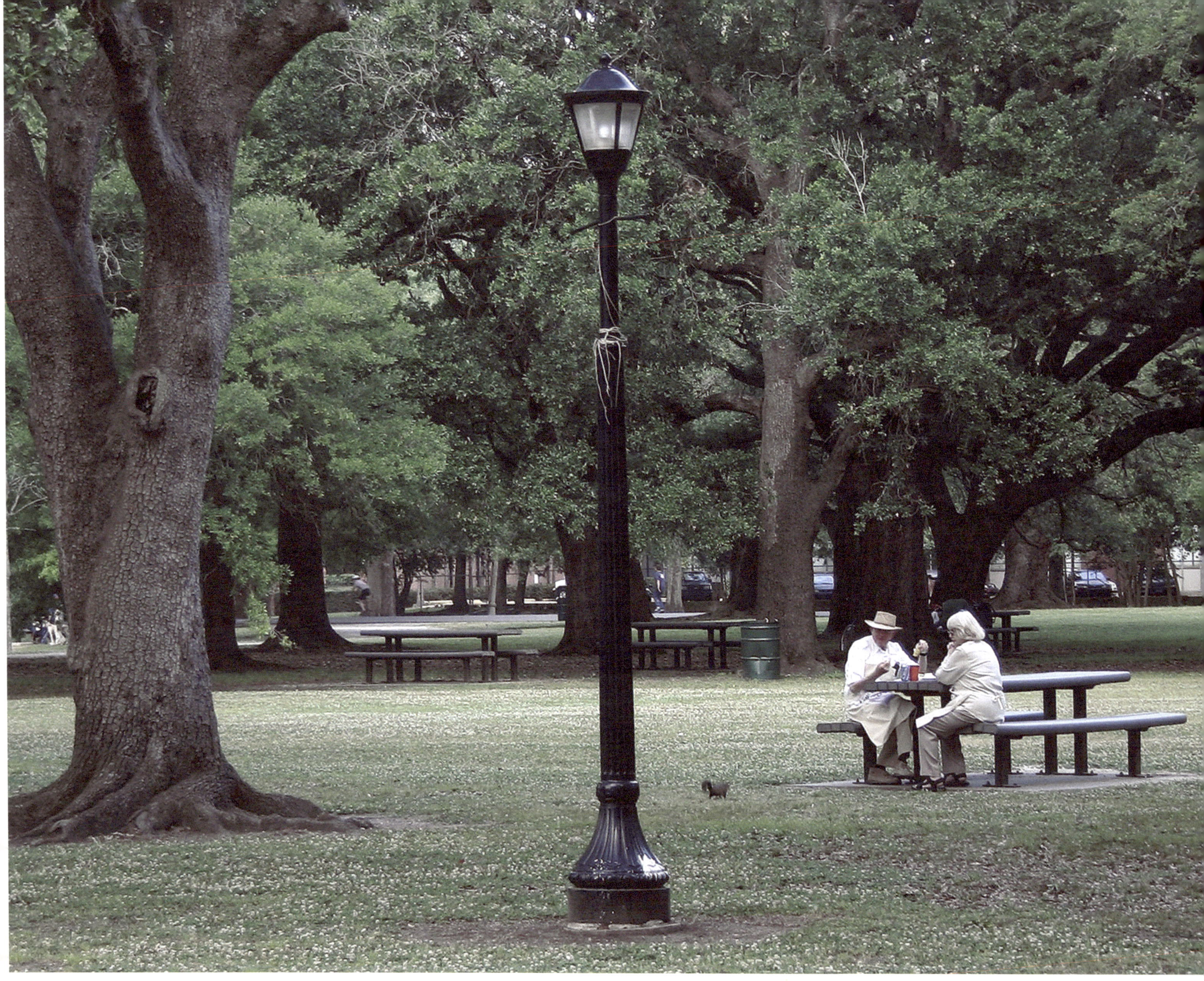

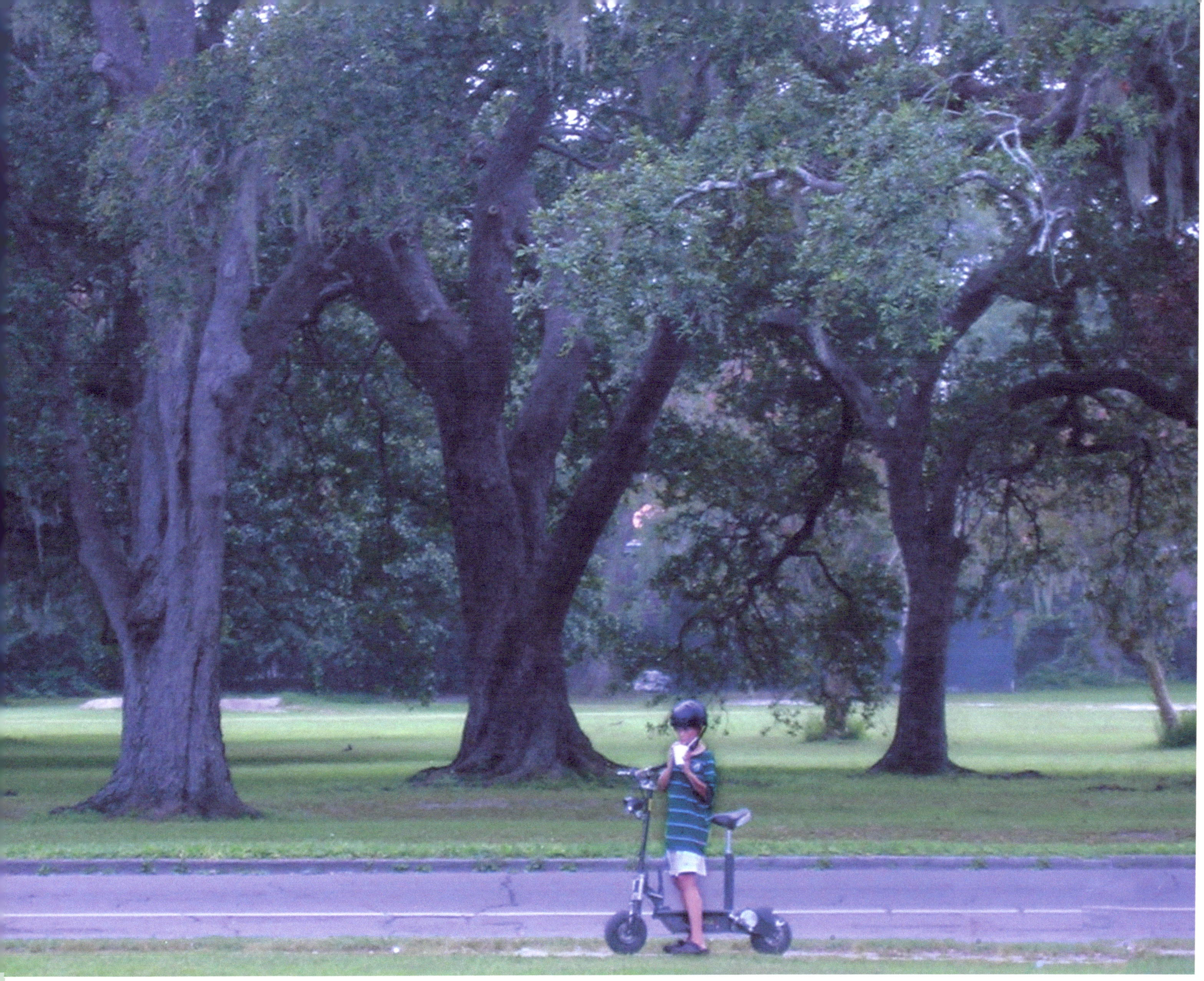

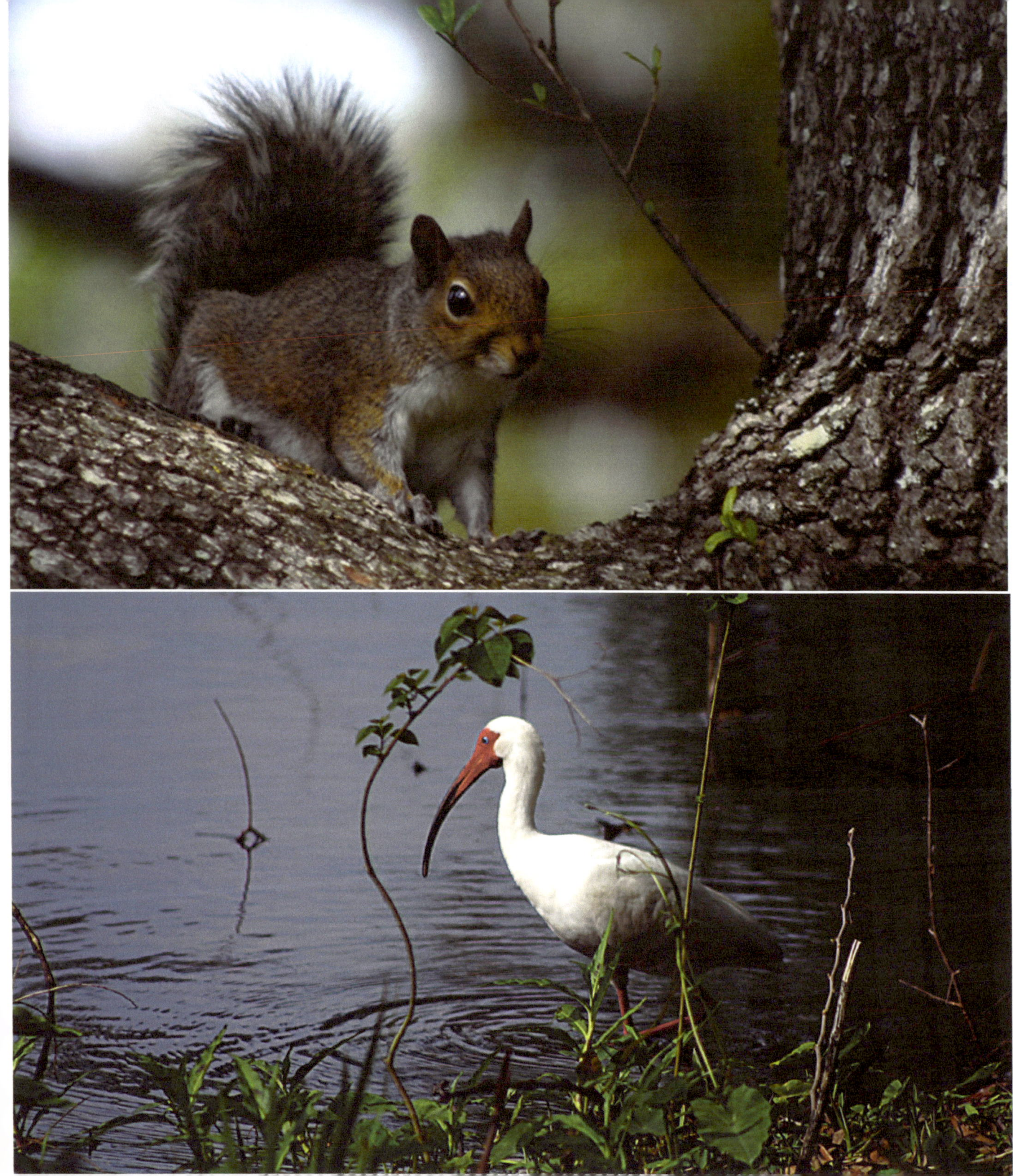

WILD

LIFE

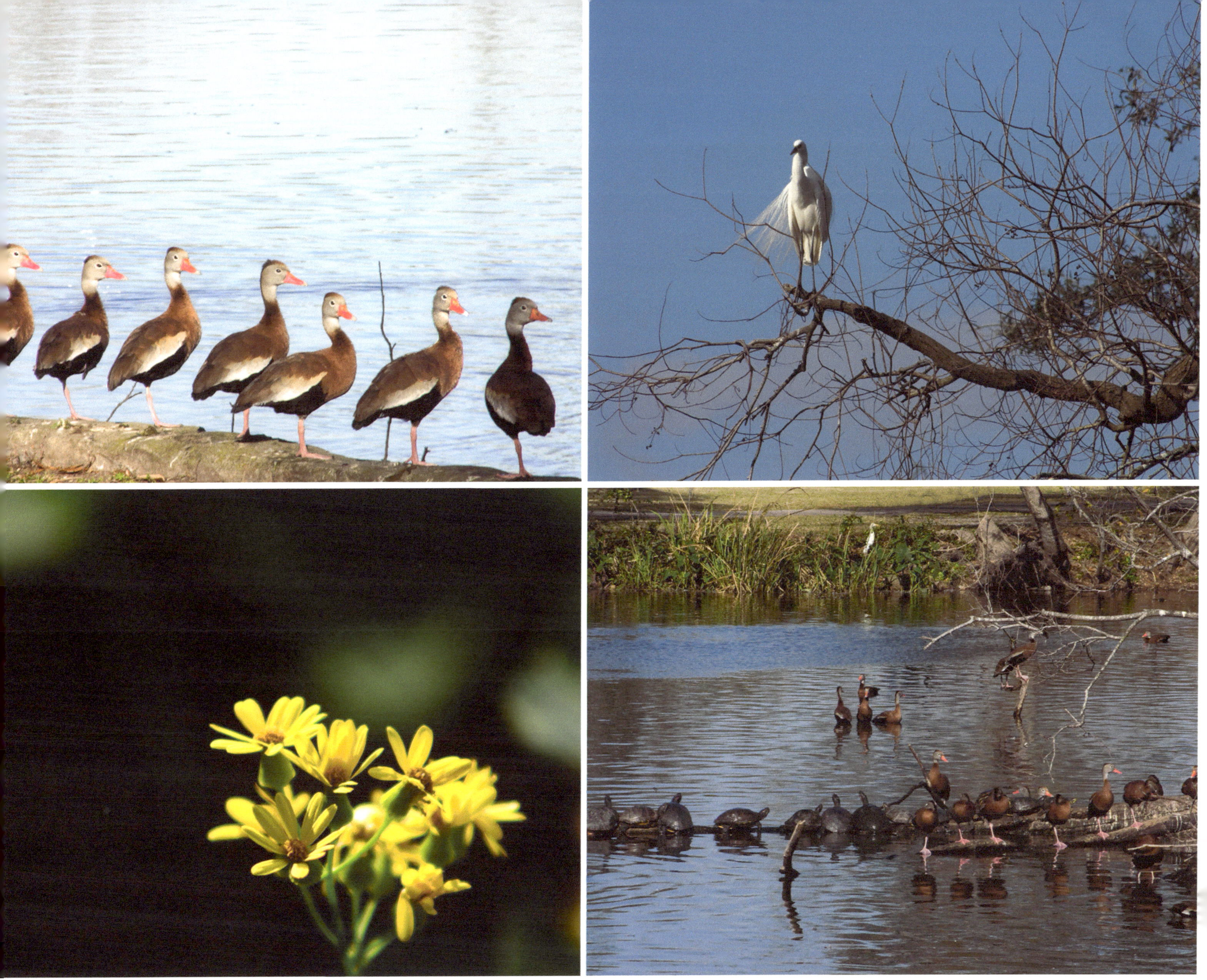

We come to sit on the lawn or climb in the trees; time for work or play. You can find places of peace and quiet in the park where you can stare-off into space and imagine that you are many worlds away; or maybe you are imagining just that that boy you saw at the mall came up smiling and started chatting. Whether you are transported to the plains of the Serengeti or to the halls of the mall, Audubon Park can provide the peace for that to happen. There can be so much strange and curious activity from parties to play to practice to power sailing to roller blading to noisy birds; still there is always space to find your peace!

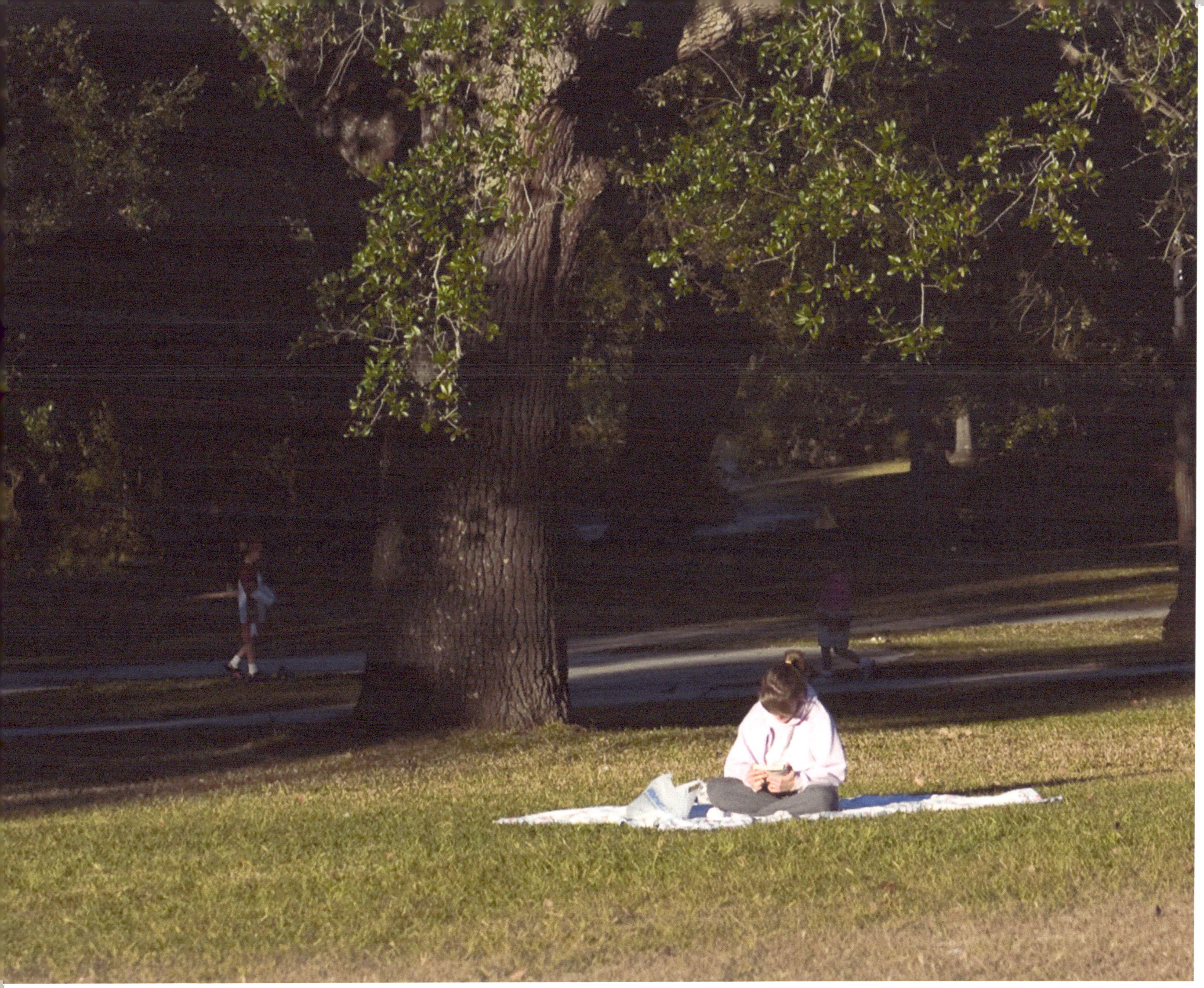

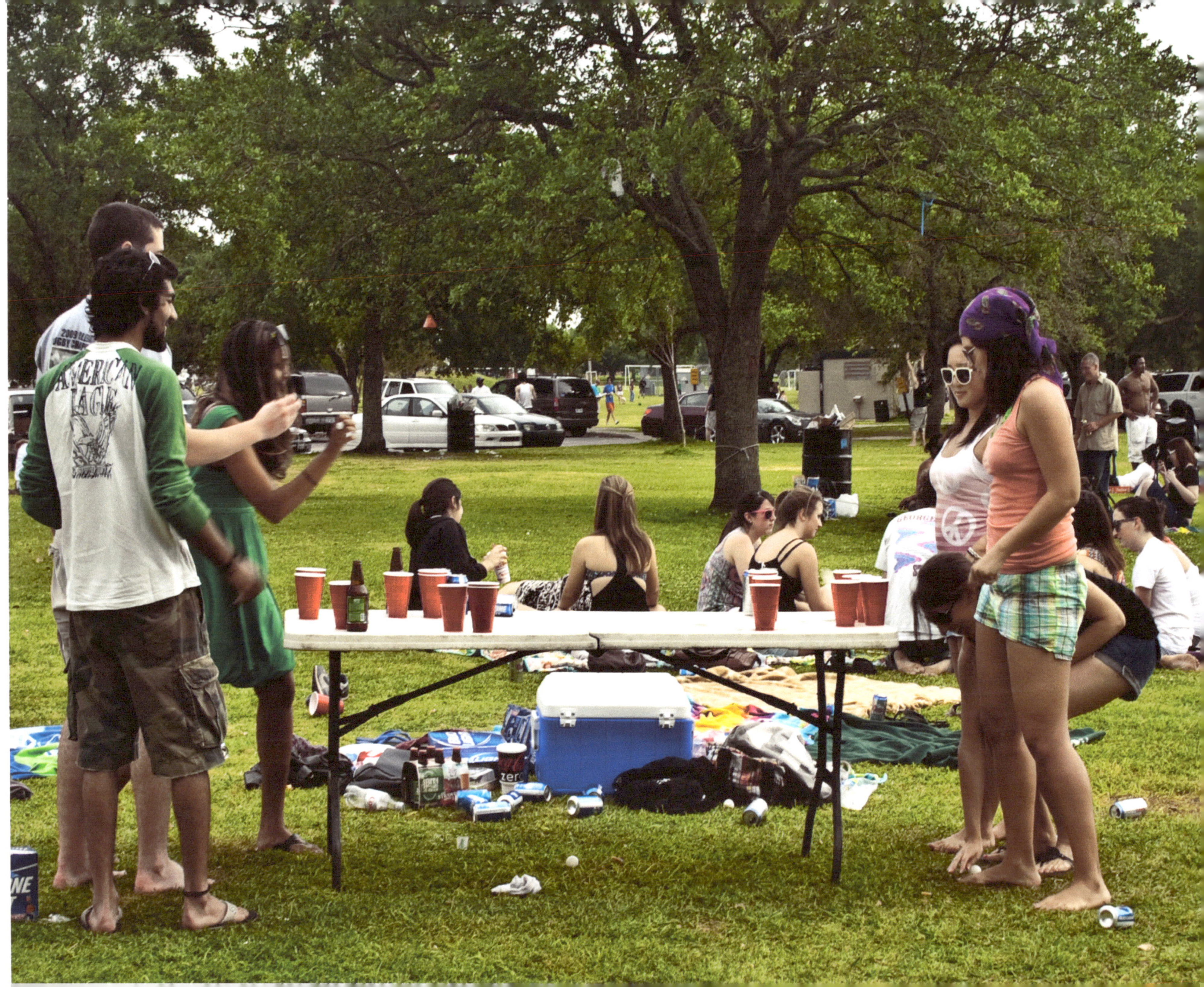

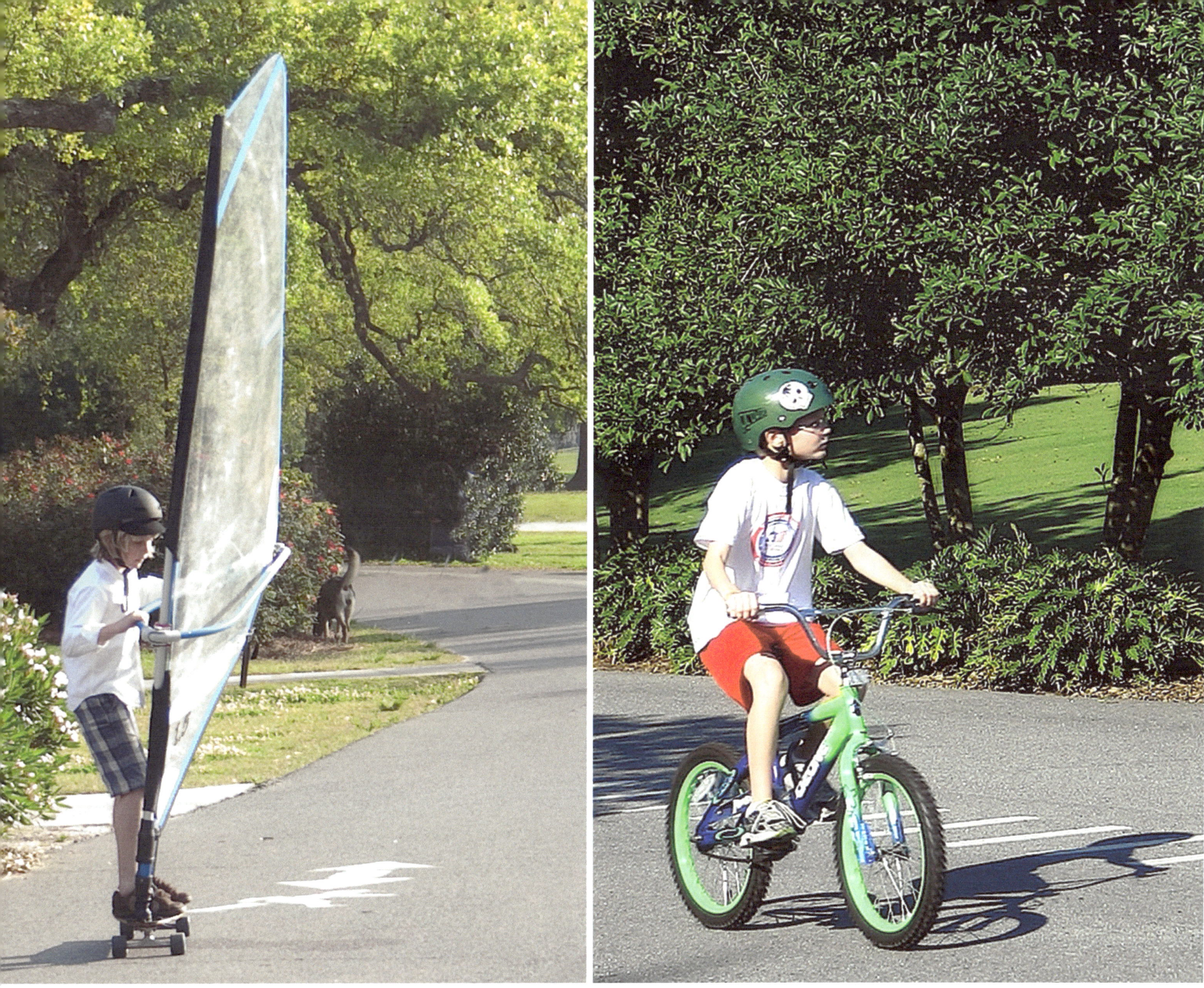

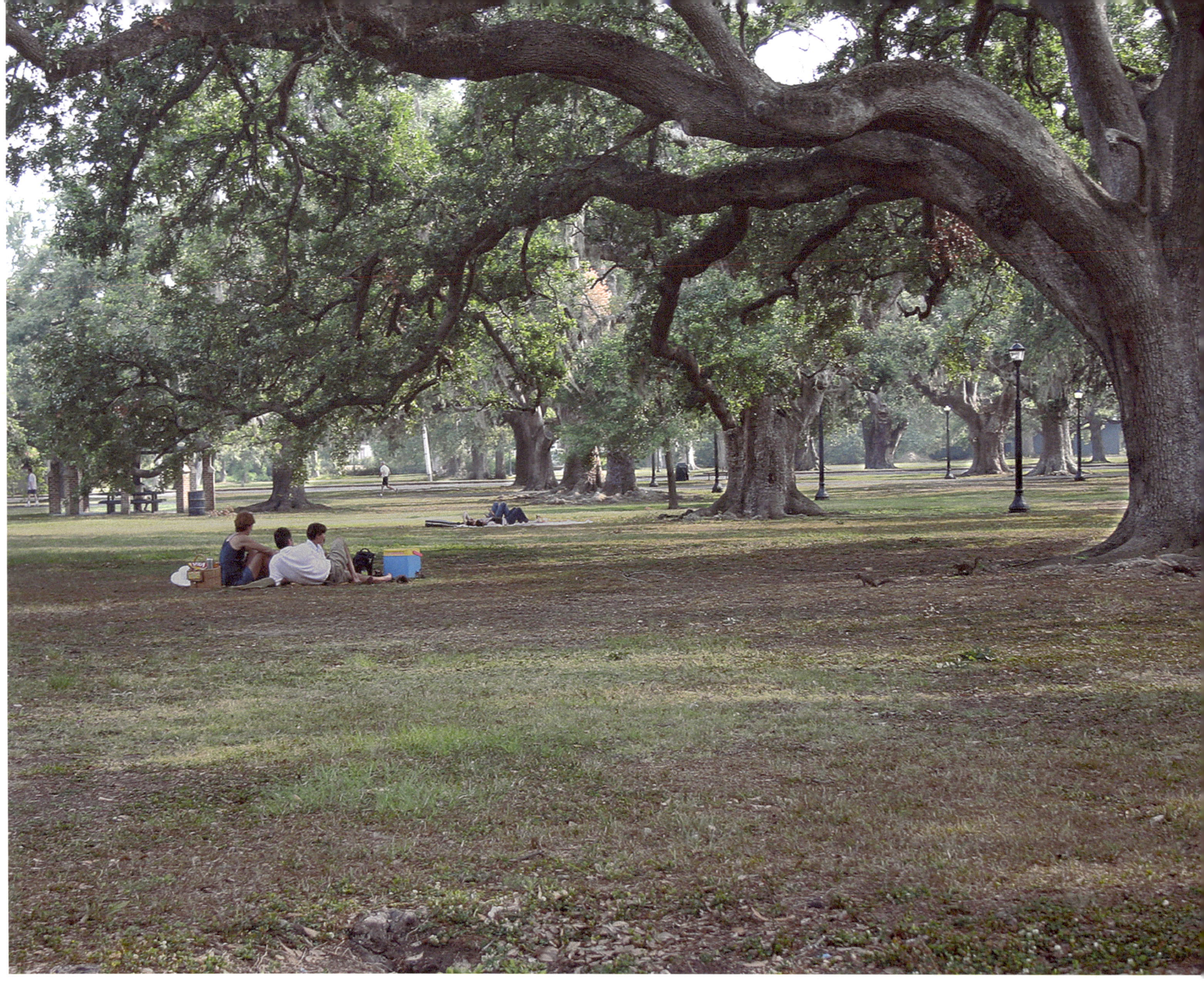

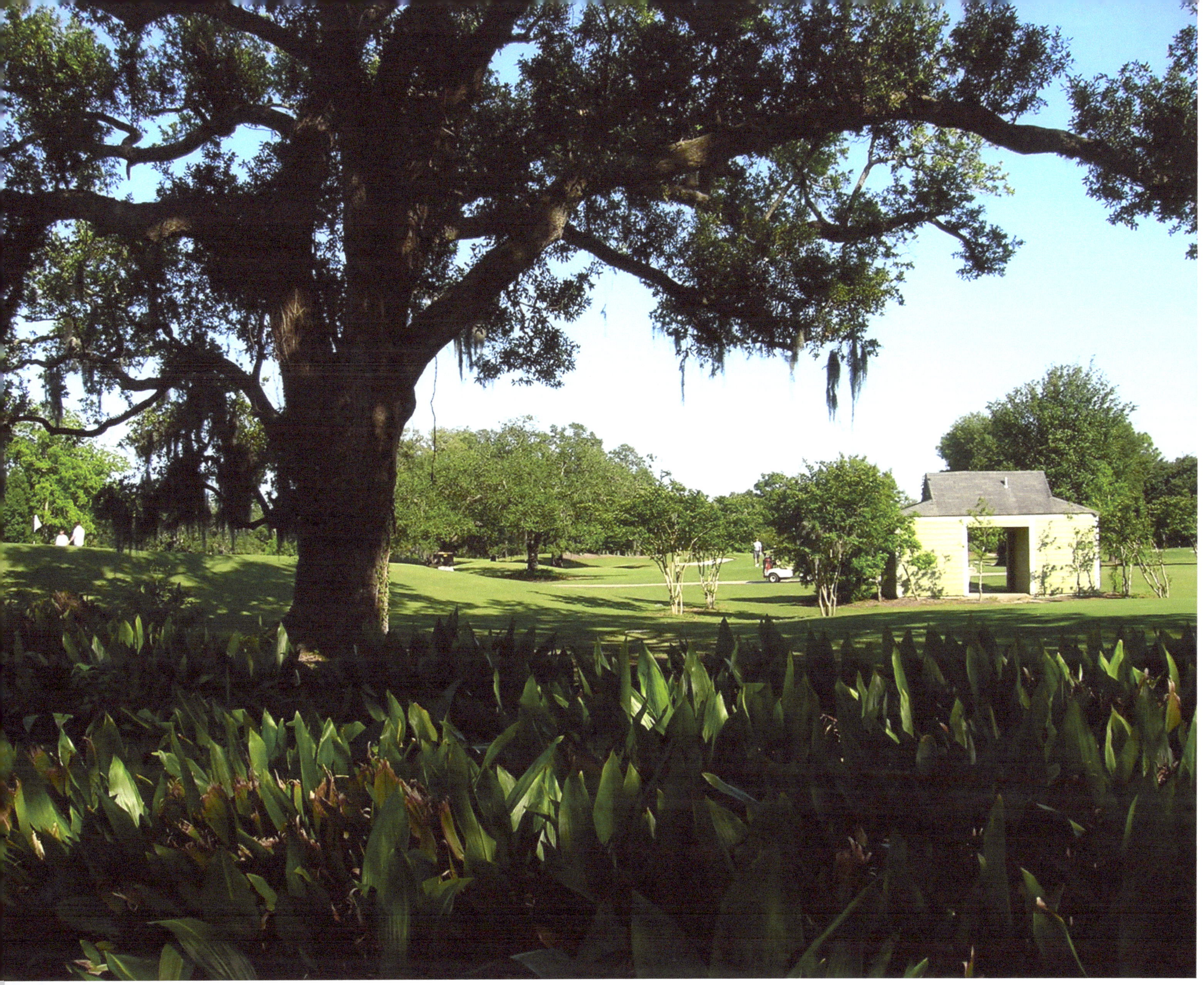

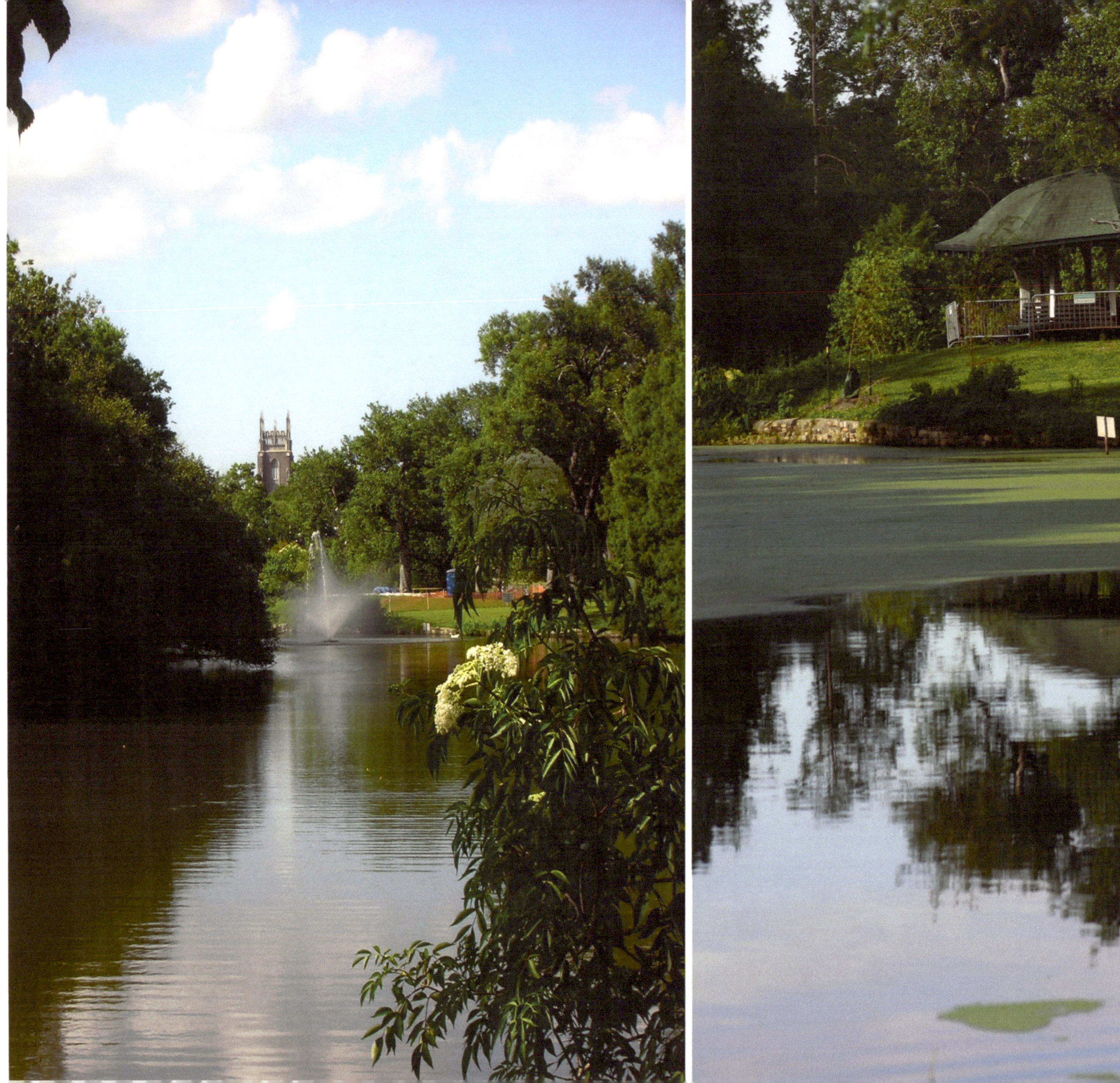

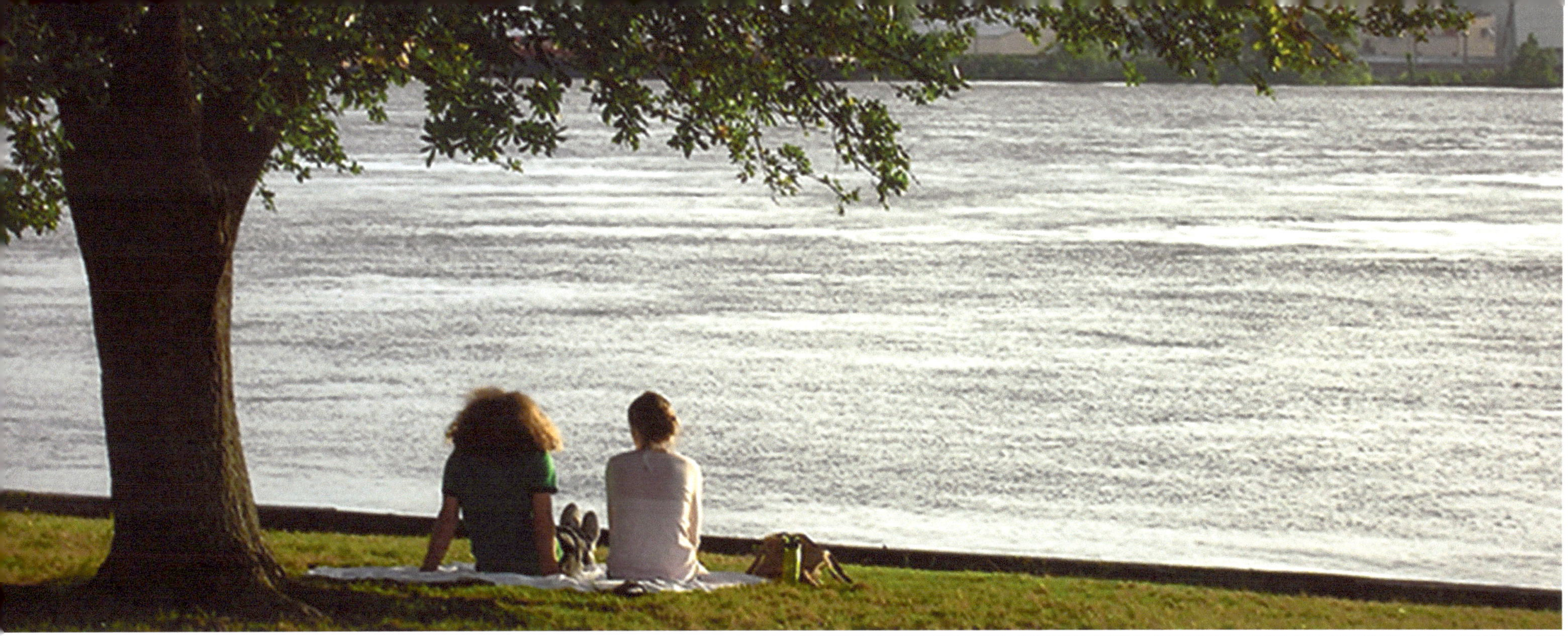

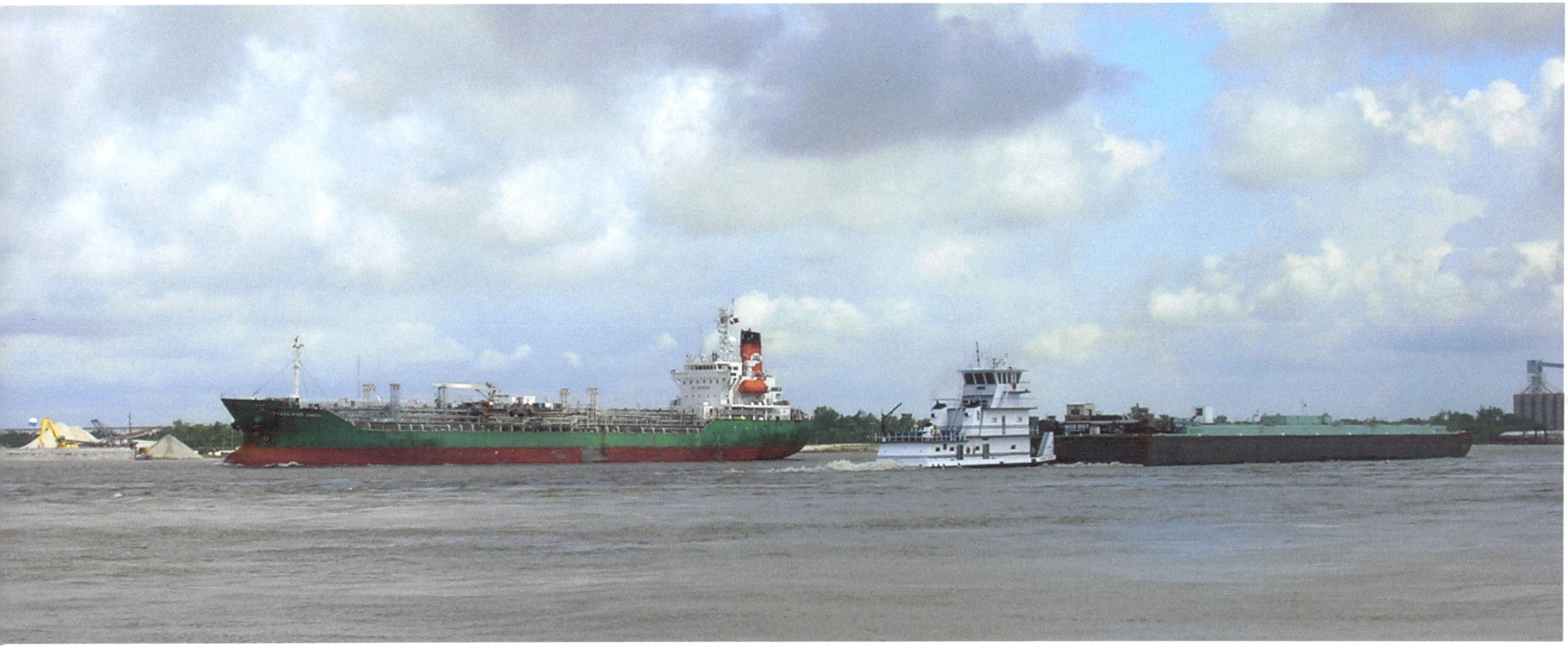

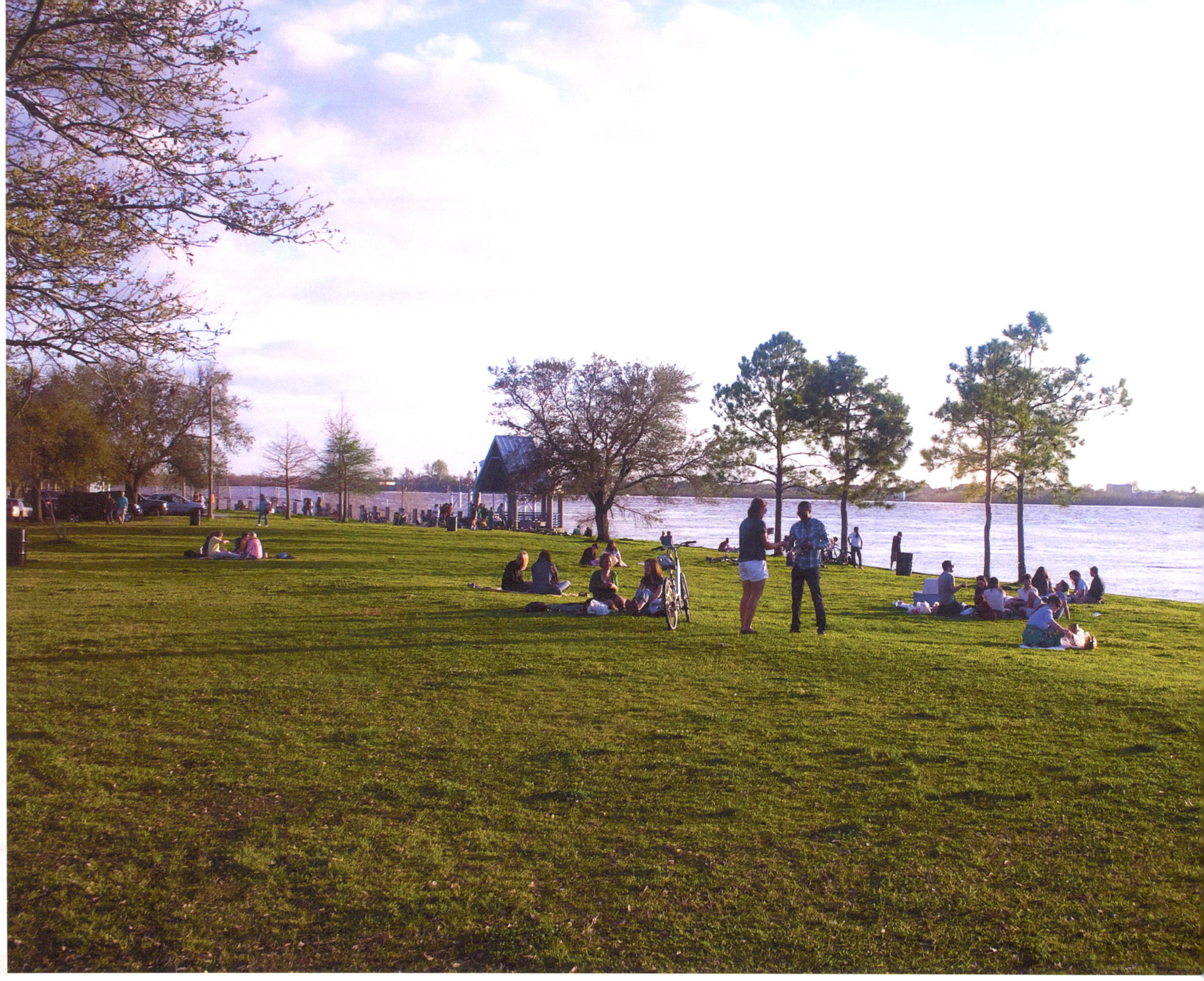

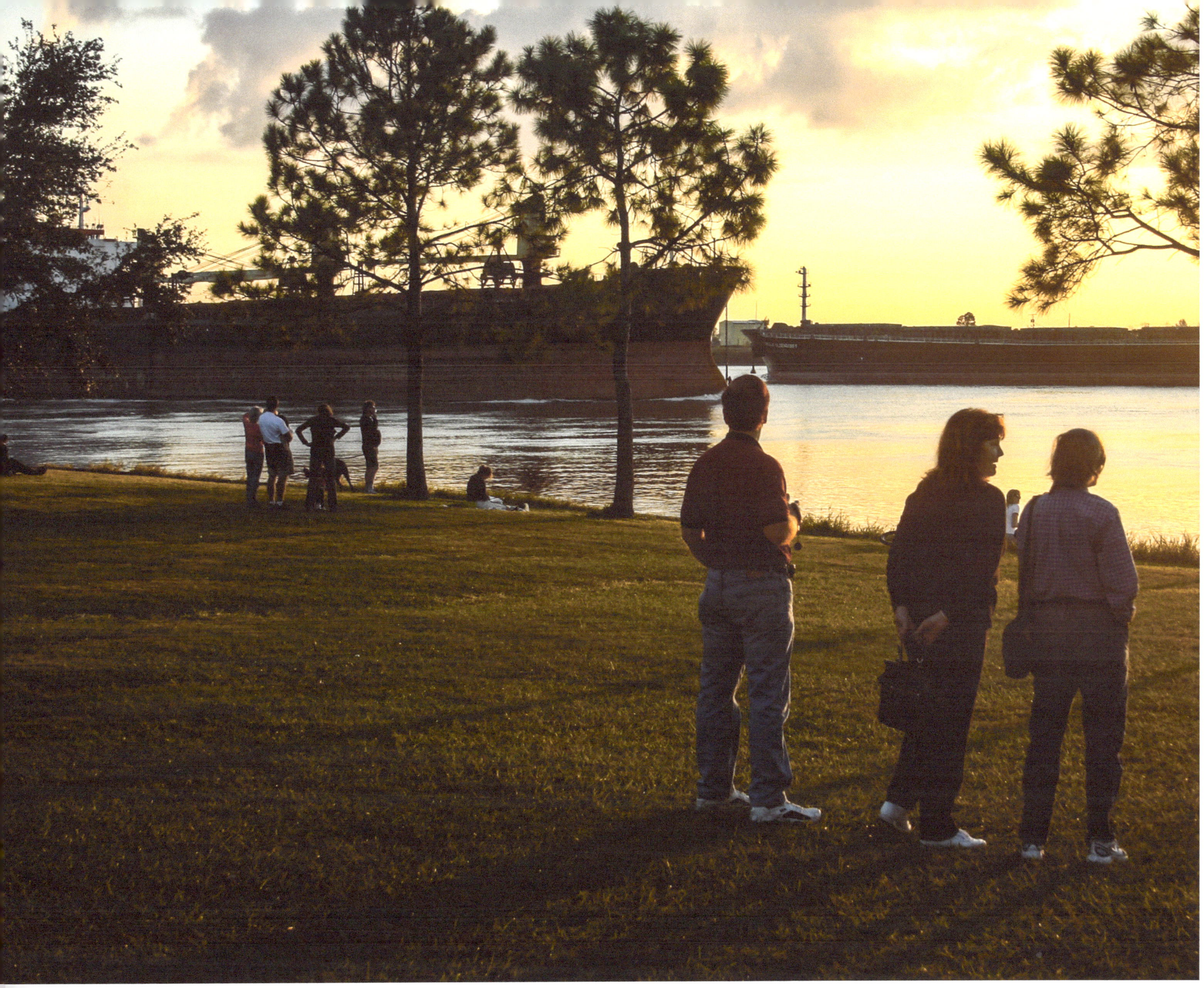